Schöningh

EinFach Englisch

L. A. Crash

... verstehen

Herausgegeben und erarbeitet von
Ulrike Klein
Gabriele Kugler-Euerle

www.schoeningh-schulbuch.de
Schöningh Verlag, Jühenplatz 1–3, 33098 Paderborn

Druck 5 4 3 2 1 / Jahr 2018 17 16 15 14
Die letzte Zahl bezeichnet das Jahr dieses Druckes.

Umschlaggestaltung: Nora Krull, Bielefeld
Druck und Bindung: westermann druck GmbH, Braunschweig

ISBN 978-3-14-041161-5

Contents

How to work with "EinFach Englisch *L.A. Crash* verstehen" 5

Approaching *L.A. Crash* 7
What makes a good film? 7
"Thumbs up" or "thumbs down" 7
Purpose and genre 7
Elements of film 10
Judging the film by its cover 12
Film posters 12
Vocab 17
The trailer 18

The film 23
A first viewing 23
The setting 24
Los Angeles – city of contrasts 25
Vocab 28
The plot 29
Scene-by-Scene analysis 30
Vocab 60
The characters and their scenarios 60
Character analysis 62
Vocab 63
About victims and victimizers 63
Vocab 81
How the characters relate 82
The soundtrack 84
Vocab 84

Writing a film review 87
Vocab 88
Possible exam tasks 91
Analysis 91
Composition 91

Appendix 92
Vocab 92
The language of film from A to Z 97
Some explanations which might help 105

Index 106

Acknowledgments 107

How to work with "EinFach Englisch *L.A. Crash* verstehen"

The purpose of this study guide is to intensify your individual understanding of the film *L.A. Crash*[1] by providing useful background knowledge and offering relevant aspects of deeper analysis.

Paul Haggis, dir. *L.A. Crash*. Universum Film 2006.

On the following pages, you will therefore find **information** on **genre** and the purpose of films in general, **summaries** of the **plot** and the **setting**, as well as **character analyses**, **explanations** of **film-related terms** and other useful **vocabulary**. These are supplemented with helpful advice for the analysis of **film posters** and **trailers** and useful tips for writing **a film review** or dealing with **exam tasks. Stop-and-think tasks** are also included to focus your attention on relevant points along the way. The **thematic vocabulary**, which is generally presented in the form of **useful chunks,** can both assist you in responding to speaking or writing tasks as well as aid your understanding of information related to the film.

As a helpful orientation, the study guide operates with a few symbols that are designed to clarify the different **functions of information and assignments**:

- [i] the **information** given here is designed to help you to understand particular aspects of the film within a larger context

[1] Please note that the film was originally published under the title *Crash*. In German-speaking countries it was shown under the title *L.A. Crash*, which is also used in this study guide.

- **assignments** have been added to help you process the information given and relate different aspects of the analysis to **your personal understanding** of the film, individual scenes or characters
- these sections exemplify aspects of **analysis** which can help you to understand **what the director or artist had in mind,** as well as providing further potentially useful vocabulary

Hoping you enjoy the film, and more importantly, wishing you every success in your work!

Approaching *L. A. Crash*

What makes a good film?

Have you ever thought about what makes a good film, an excellent film, a blockbuster?

Think of a good film you have seen recently and give three reasons why you particularly liked it.

Do your reasons relate to the genre of the film, its theme and/or the actors in it?

"Thumbs up" or "thumbs down"

Anyone who watches a film can be considered a **film critic** of sorts and his or her particular perception can therefore be regarded as accurate. Since the quality of a film cannot be measured scientifically, and its artistic greatness therefore cannot be rated or quantified objectively, the judgment of films generally comes down to **personal taste and individual experience**. Nevertheless, in explaining why we like a film or not, it can be helpful to consider certain criteria that are commonly used by critics, reviewers, award lists and opinion polls to answer the question of why one particular film gets excellent reviews and possibly becomes a blockbuster while another is torn to pieces by the critics and ends up a box office flop.

Purpose and genre

When creating films, there are various aims that directors and producers may choose to pursue in their art. Typically, however, their principal aim is to **provoke a strong reac-**

tion in their audience. To this end, they may choose to create films which

- captivate and entertain
- educate and engage
- illustrate human experience
- alter awareness
- inform, involve, and inspire
- make the audience laugh, cry
- shock and provoke thought
- …

Purpose and **genre** are often closely related because the **effect** achieved by a film can be one of the characteristics of its genre. Nevertheless, films can also be categorized in many other different ways, for example, with regard to **target audience**, **setting**, **theme/topic**, **format** or **genre**, as in the following list:

▷ For each of the following genres, think of films that you have watched. Reflect upon which aspects of the genre help you to describe why you enjoyed watching them.

Genres	are/depict
Action	• fast paced • physical stunts and chases • rescues, battles, fights, escapes, destructive crises • often one-dimensional heroes and villains *(good guy – bad guy)*
Adventure	• searches for the unknown • journeys to exotic locations • "jungle" and "desert" epics
Animated	(not strictly related to genre but more to technique) • often designed to appeal most strongly to children • animals and/or usually inanimate objects become evil villains or heroes

Genres	are/depict
Comedy	• light-hearted plots designed to amuse the audience and provoke laughter • exaggerated situations, language, action, relationships and characters • some different types: *slapstick*, *screwball*, *spoofs* and *parodies*, *romantic comedies*, *black comedy*
Crime	• fast paced with an air of mystery • actions of a criminal mastermind versus the rise and fall of sinister criminals
Documen-tary	• non-fictional • "slice of life" reporting on an issue of interest
Drama	• serious and plot-driven • real-life characters, settings, situations, and stories involving intense character development and interaction • strong human emotions • usually not focused on special effects
Fantasy	• imaginative and fantastic themes • fairy-tale adventures or plots from the Dark Ages • magic, supernatural events
Horror	• large amount of violence and gore in the plot • arousal of the audience's worst fears and nightmares about the arrival of an evil force, person, or event • mythical creatures, such as ghosts, vampires, and zombies
Romance	• varying tone from happy to tragic • love between two protagonists, e.g. *love at first sight, forbidden love, love triangles, and love requiring great sacrifices*

Genres	are/depict
Science Fiction	• hypothetical, science-based • outer-space adventures and extra-terrestrial encounters • futuristic elements and technological advances that raise important social, political, and philosophical issues • usually set in the future, either on Earth or in space
Suspense/ Mystery	• a person of authority, usually a detective, trying to solve a mysterious crime • clues, investigation, and logical reasoning • "whodunit" suspense created through visual cues or unusual plot twists

Elements of film

Obviously, within each of these genres, there are also other more detailed criteria that can help us to argue for or against a film.

▷ For each aspect, tick those elements which you believe make a film great.
Which films can you quote to support your opinion?

Ideas and script

- ☐ a meaningful and engaging plot that not only tells an intriguing and unusual story, but also makes the viewers change their perspective and/or moves them deeply
- ☐ a plot that illustrates important reality-based themes related to *good and evil, love, loyalty*, etc.
- ☐ people portrayed as they are in real-world settings and confronted with controversial themes
- ☐ a central conflict that is well developed without containing elements that are repetitive or predictable
- ☐ believable and plausible actions and interactions

- ☐ well-written dialogues
- ☐ a profound message, moral or ethic which echoes in the viewer's mind
- ☐ subject matter viewed from a different, unexpected or individualistic angle that avoids clichéd ideas
- ☐ attention-grabbing scenes from the very first shot without lengthy introductions
- ☐ original ending that leaves the audience feeling content

Characters and actors

- ☐ intriguing "good guys" and villains
- ☐ simple people from real life
- ☐ characters the audience can believe in, who act in plausible ways
- ☐ convincing actors who make us empathize with and care about what happens to the characters
- ☐ rich characterization in multiple meaningful scenes
- ☐ characters who evoke profound emotions

Style and technique

- ☐ comprehensible follow-up
- ☐ scenery that is pleasing to the eye and emphasizes the themes and moods of the film without being distracting
- ☐ appropriate mise en scène for the setting and props reflecting the period and atmosphere of the film
- ☐ good sound and lighting that allows the audience to clearly see and hear everything significant while at the same time creating the appropriate mood for the scene
- ☐ unobtrusive but effective camera work; creative camera angles
- ☐ effective and creative transitions between scenes
- ☐ sound(track) that compliments the visuals and conveys the emotion of the scene

Overall effect

I think a great film …

- ☐ is one that pulls you into a new world, capturing your mind and soul
- ☐ can make the unbelievable believable
- ☐ sends chills down your spine and keeps you glued to your seat
- ☐ engages you from beginning to end
- ☐ connects everyone to everyone else
- ☐ makes everyone experience the same emotion at the same time
- ☐ conveys real human truth

▷ Note that the criteria given above have a lot of specific vocabulary to offer, so it is a good idea to collect the expressions that you find useful in a network.

Judging the film by its cover

Film posters

How do we become aware of a film that might interest us? In addition to **recommendations** from friends, there are various forms of **film advertising**, such as **trailers, sneak-previews, print ads, radio and TV spots**, or **posters,** which may attract our attention.

Film posters advertising an upcoming film are prominently **displayed on** billboards, in the lobby of local film theaters, in magazines, on the Internet, as well as on or around public transport, for example, on the sides of buses or in subway stations. The aim of such posters is to let future audiences know that a new **film is due for release**.

As a form of **promotion** that is often seen only very briefly, a film poster has to provide a range of information in an eye-catching form. Below are some examples of the information that is typically included.

- film title in a big and bold font
- powerful and attractive images of the film's starring actors
- film classification details (e.g. age suitability)
- memorable tagline(s)/brief one-line summary of what the film is about
- mention of awards won by the director, producer or actor for previous films
- praise in the form of one-line reviews, recommendations and ratings
- impressive billing block (the cast/crew of the film, producers, distributor and financier behind the film)
- the release date

Obviously, all of these elements are designed to **raise awareness** and, in doing so, to **generate hype**. The **images and graphics** that are used for a poster hint at the **genre** and **narrative** that the film will follow, and the **designs, colors and fonts** reflect the **tone** of the film. In this way, the **target viewer** is given an insight into what the film may be about.

▷ Take a look at the promotional poster or DVD cover for the film *L. A. Crash* (p. 14). What kind of film do you expect to see? What might the film be about? Do you know any of the actors? If so, from which film(s)? Does this affect your motivation to see the film?

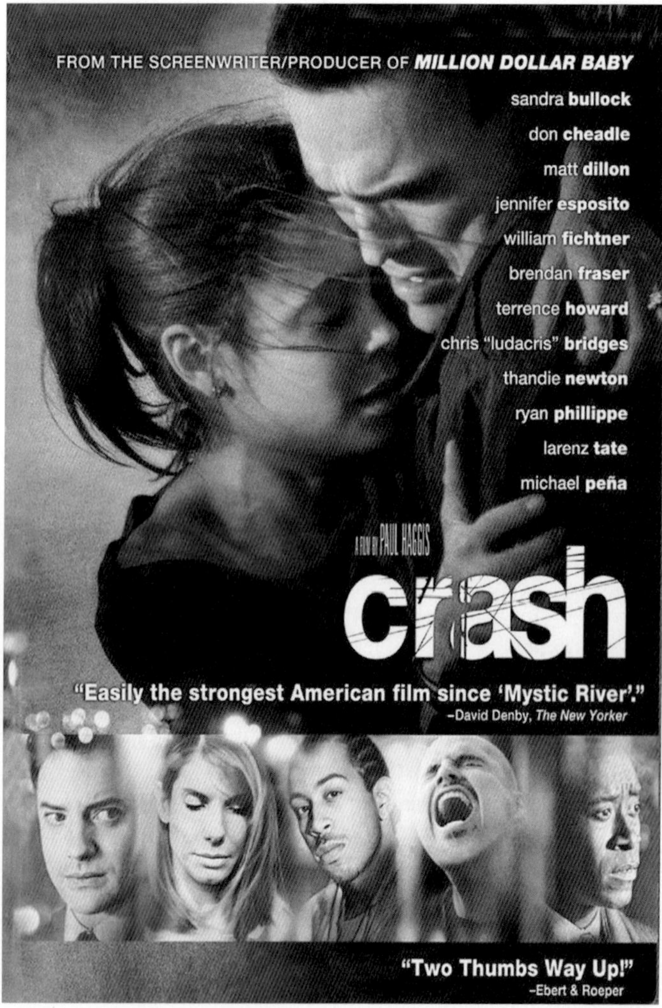

Find other film posters for *L. A. Crash* on the Internet and use the questions and example on p. 15 to examine them. To what extent do they convey the same message as the poster analysed here?

When analysing promotional posters for *L.A.Crash*, the following questions may come in handy:

a) Does the design of the poster
- give the viewer an idea about the content of the film?
- feature the film title prominently?
- show the film's main actors?
- reflect the mood and tone of the film?

b) Which other devices are used to persuade the viewer to go and see the film?
- colors and their connotations
- objects and symbols
- taglines/slogans
- etc.

▷ Now read the following analysis and highlight 5 important aspects that are included.

Analysis of a film poster
When looking at the poster, the central image of a man and a woman and the title of the film in white block letters immediately seem to connect and become the focus of attention. In the center of the poster, a light-skinned, black woman is clinging to a white man, who is holding her tightly. Her face seems to be showing anguish, pain or grief, as though she has just experienced a crisis situation. The further expression of relief that can be read in her body language and her face is most probably connected to the man who is comforting her. The image of crisscrossing lines or wires in the white bold letters of the title and the out-of-focus headlights in the background of the image could be clues that she has just been rescued after a car crash. With her arms around the man's neck, a wedding ring clearly visible on the far right of the im-

age, and her head nestling in a trusting way against his shoulder, their embrace seems intimate and caring. The brownish colors used to shade the two of them convey a sense of responsibility and support and echo the man's expression of concern and determination. The contrast of the soft and blurry aqua-colored background emphasizes the idea of protection and atonement. Although the viewer may be starting to wonder whether these two people are the protagonists in a romantic drama, the long list of actors' names on the right and the five images of further characters at the bottom automatically raise the question of how these people of different ethnic and social backgrounds may be connected to each other and to the film. Their faces show a multitude of emotions: distrust, sadness, resignation, aggression, pride, despair or consternation, all of which strongly suggest to the viewer that the drama that the film depicts is not focused on the two people in the center alone. The credit and critics' praise finally serve to convince the viewer that this film by (the not yet acclaimed) director Paul Haggis will be more than worth their while.

The following section presents additional information on the **meanings of colors** and some vocabulary which might help you to write an analysis of your own.

The Connotations of Colors

Red: the color of blood and fire, suggesting rage and anger, power and passion, love and desire, danger and war

Yellow: the color of sunshine associated with joy and happiness, honor and loyalty

Green: the color of nature symbolizes growth and freshness, fertility and safety
Blue: the color of the sky and the sea, often suggests truth and stability, trust and loyalty, confidence and faith
Brown: the color of the Earth, typically evokes physical comfort and quality, reliability and trustworthiness
White: the color of purity and virginity, often associated with innocence and goodness, perfection and cleanliness
Black: the color of darkness, evokes fear and the unknown, suggests mystery and evil, but also formality and elegance

from "The Meaning of Colors" by Raetta Parker, https://resources.oncourse.iu.edu/access/content/user/rreagan/Filemanager_Public_Files/meaningofcolors.htm, 2002 [13.03.2014];

Vocab

Film posters	
Layout	• detailed/simple • main focus of the layout is/the poster is split in two/the layout separates … from …/the layout is well spread out/the layout places emphasis on • the edges are blackened/blurred • in the foreground/background/center/on the left/right/at the bottom/top of …
Image	• key image/main image/the image in focus/the image taking up the most space • realistic/edited/focused/blurry/blocked • to depict/show/portray/represent/illustrate/convey
Colors	• black-and-white/colored/a color palette varying from … to … • realistic/surreal/edited • the colors contrast/emphasize/suggest/blend into one another/(sharply) separate … from …

Film posters	
Text	• title – credits – tagline/slogan – billing block (text at the bottom of a film poster giving more detailed information about the film and its cast and crew) • cast (all actors in a film or play) – crew (all the people involved behind the scenes in making a film or play) – director – producer • have the leading role/feature/star/act in a film • genre: drama/comedy/thriller/mystery/science fiction • positioned at the top/bottom/edge/on the right/left/in the center/dominate/be the focus of attention • in small/large lettering/font size – big/small/highly-condensed typeface – large/bold/italic type – capital letters
Viewer's reaction	• focus attention on/draw the eye to/divert/distract attention from/catch the viewer's interest/make the viewer focus on • make the viewer wonder why/believe/think/hope/fear • intrigue the viewer with/by/the viewer naturally assumes … • … suggest that/evoke a sense of …/signal to the viewer

The trailer

We are moving forward

Another way to approach a film is by watching its **trailer**, which is yet another type of **advertisement**. You can find the trailer for *L. A. Crash* on:
www.youtube.com/watch?v=durNwe9pL0E

Have the expectations that were raised by the film title or poster been confirmed? Can you explain why or why not? Any surprises? Any questions?

▷ Tick which functions and characteristics from the list below are incorporated in the trailer to *L. A. Crash*.

Function of trailers in general:

- ☐ arouse interest in the film
- ☐ present the cast
- ☐ reach out to target audience
- ☐ inform about classification (viewing restrictions) of film

Characteristics:

- ☐ short
- ☐ repeated show of title
- ☐ key scenes revealing central theme/conflict/plot
- ☐ short shots, quick cuts, cliffhangers
- ☐ powerful dialogue
- ☐ voiceover
- ☐ on-screen texts
- ☐ hints as to genre

In addition to these aspects, the trailer to *L. A. Crash* includes the following features:

- ☑ The film's classification: Rated R (in America) for language, sexual content and some violence. Viewers must be 12 years or older.
- ☑ Trailer company credits
- ☑ Voiceover and on-screen texts
- ☑ "directed and co-written by academy award nominee paul haggis"
- ☑ Title
- ☑ Cast
- ☑ Billing block
- ☑ "Coming Soon"

Transcripts of voiceover …

It's the sense of touch.

In any real city, you walk, you know, you brush past people, people bump into you. In L.A., no one touches you …

We're always behind this metal and glass.

… and on-screen text

we are searching for an answer
we are moving forward
we are coming together
we are falling apart
when you're moving at the speed of life
we are bound to collide with each other

It's the sense of touch.

I think we miss that touch so much, that we crash into each other just so that we can feel something.

transcribed from the trailer: www.crashfilm.com, 2005

▷ Mark 10 expressions from the analysis below which might help you to talk about the trailer for 3 minutes. In a short presentation, explain what impact the trailer has on you and whether it makes you want to see the film.

Analysis of the trailer

The trailer for *L.A. Crash* presents brief glimpses that are related to the film's primary themes of arbitrary aggression (violence, anger, hatred, crime, abuse of authority by the police, intimidation) and complex human ties (healthy relationships and destructive conflicts between father and daughter, mother and son, husband and wife, colleagues, friends, ethnic groups and different social classes). These glimpses of seemingly unrelated situations serve to give the viewer a taste of some of the basic concepts that the film is built upon: scenes of modern city life, in which diverse characters (couples, police officers, a girl and her father) love, hate, suffer and rejoice. Synthesizer music, a random array of sounds and a crescendo of dialogue that erupts in shots, which are then followed by a melancholic melody, all help to create an atmosphere of drama and suspense. At the same time, the general mood seems to be one of resignation due to a constant alternation between despair and hope. The voiceover with its reserved tone establishes the setting and relates the title to the central plot of people *crashing* into one another, while the simple statements of the on-screen-texts hint at the complex themes of interpersonal conflict and communication breakdowns following or underlying the collisions. All in all, the trailer addresses a target audience that enjoys drama based on human relationships and suspense.

▷ Now that you have had a closer look at the film posters and the trailer, why not try recollecting the central ideas that you remember in an *acrostic* to finalize this section. You can then compare this acrostic to one that you do after you have thoroughly analysed the film.

C

R

A

S

H

L. A. Crash
Release date: 2004 Toronto International Film Festival
Country: USA
Cert (UK): 15
Germany:
USA: rated R
(under 17 requires accompanying parent or adult guardian). It has violence, strong language (including many racial slurs) and a brief sex scene.
Runtime: 112 mins
Director: Paul Haggis
Producers: Paul Haggis, Mark R. Harris, Bobby Moresco, Don Cheadle, Bob Yari, Cathy Schulman
Screenplay: Paul Haggis
Cast: Don Cheadle, Matt Dillon, Sandra Bullock, Thandie Newton among others
Budget: $ 6.5 million
Box office: $ 98,410,061

The film

A first viewing

When watching the film for the first time, you may want to record some ideas reflecting your spontaneous reactions, which you can later compare to your findings after a deeper analysis of the film.

- How did the film make you feel while you were watching it and after it ended? Did you like how you felt?
- Which scene/image will stay with you for a long time? What effect did it have on you when you first saw it and what effect does it have on you now?
- Which character in the film did you like best/least? Why?
- Which questions has the film raised for you? Where do you expect to find an answer?
- Which other film(s)/book(s)/real-life situation(s) do certain scenes from *L.A. Crash* remind you of? Which similarities and differences can you see?
- Which would you consider to be the 5 most important problems this film deals with? How do they relate to your life?
- Which questions would you like to ask the director or one of the actors?
- What would you have done differently with/in the film and why?

You might like to use some of the following sentence starters to talk or write about your viewing experience.

The film deals with/is about …

For me, the best/most fascinating/scariest/most terrible/most irritating scene was the one where …

I personally liked it best when …

I felt sad/worried/shocked/horrified/angry/embarrassed/ confused/irritated when …
I hated the moment when …/found the scene most unrealistic in which …
I still wonder/cannot understand why … – I accept/ comprehend/tolerate that …
The part I could best/least relate to was the one where/ when …
I am still touched by …/in a state of shock because …

The setting

The Canadian director **Paul Haggis**, who was actually born in London in 1953, began his career in the film industry by directing and producing television shows before eventually becoming a **screenwriter and filmmaker**. As the founder of *Artists for Peace and Justice*, Haggis was strongly **committed to social concerns** until he was carjacked in Hancock Park – an affluent residential neighborhood of Los Angeles. At that point, he realized that his view of things had been highly subjective. In writing the screenplay for the film *L. A. Crash*, which won him Academy Awards for Best Picture and Best Original Screenplay, he was trying to come to terms with the **complex mix of emotions** that he felt after the attack.

The following quote expresses which **purpose** he was hoping to realize through the film: "I was trying to talk about where we are right now as a society, and talk about the fear we all live in, and certainly since 9-11, how it's affected us and the world."

Haggis decided to integrate his personal story into the **wider context** of the multifaceted city of Los Angeles.

Read more about Haggis' carjacking experience on:
www.landmarktheatres.com/mn/crash.html

Los Angeles – city of contrasts

Screenshot taken from *L. A. Crash*

When we think of Los Angeles, we usually conjure up images of the **laid-back** California **lifestyle**, the **glamour** of stars living in Hollywood or Beverly Hills, large sandy beaches and surf spots in Malibu or Santa Monica, high-end shopping in the Westside or first-class leisure activities in the Valley or the San Bernardino Mountains. In short, L.A. seems to be **a city offering a multitude of possibilities** for everyone to make a life and **echoing the promises of the American Dream**.
In *L. A. Crash*, however, our attention is directed to a less-glamorous side of Los Angeles, with the film showing us **scenes of poverty, neglect, crime and violence**. These aspects create an atmosphere of bitter **inequality**, which in turn nourishes **envy** and **distrust**, **racial intolerance** and **human suffering**, all of which simmers dangerously under the city's dazzling surface.
Looking at L. A. from the perspective of race relations certainly paints this very different picture of a **segregated, urban community** in trouble. Ongoing and above-average population growth has caused considerable demographic changes over the past 30 years: the percentage of

whites living in Los Angeles county has dropped from 47.8 % in 1980 to 27.3 % in 2013, whereas the number of Hispanics has nearly doubled, now representing 48.2 % (census 2013) of the urban population. At the same time, the decrease of the overall black population (16.7 % in 1980 to 9.3 % in 2013), due in part to an upwardly-mobile black middle class, means that today immigrants from Mexico or Central America live in the former centers of black culture. As a result, Spanish is now often the only language heard on the streets of South Central.

An important consequence of such **racial divides** is that they create a constantly-changing tapestry of fragmented city blocks, in which drastically-different worlds produce **distinct cultures, values and lifestyles**. Since the borders of these ethnically-shaped neighborhoods are not clearly defined, these different cultures are in **daily confrontation** with each other: in particular, the perceived opportunities and advantages of the other ethnicities are under permanent scrutiny, which often leads to **competition and resentment**, and occasionally culminates in **eruptions of violence**. A good example of this can be seen in the Rodney King Riots, in which more than fifty people died and over 2,000 were injured, and which left countless communities devastated.

In 1991, the African-American Rodney King had been pulled over by Los Angeles police officers (LAPD) for speeding. Despite a videotape showing four police officers verbally abusing and brutally beating and kicking King, an all-white jury acquitted the officers a year later. The **riots** first started in South Los Angeles before spreading to other areas within a six-day period. Not only did the reputation of administrative institutions (police, law system) suffer greatly as a result of the Rodney King case, but it also became apparent that the question of how other factors, like **education, business initiatives, welfare programs**, etc. could more effectively contribute to a more **equal and unified multicultural America** in the future had (and still has) not been answered.

Furthermore, ever since the **9/11 terrorist attacks on the World Trade Center** by the Islamic terrorist group Al-Qaeda, **fear and a growing sense of insecurity** have further **fuelled racial bigotry** in parts of American society and impacted the life and experience of ethnic minorities, in particular Arab Muslims, who previously aroused little attention. Government statistics have shown an increase in reports of **racial profiling, verbal assault, workplace discrimination, threats to safety** or even **hate crimes** among the American Muslim population.

These are the realities Paul Haggis chooses to confront in his film. By focusing his audience's attention on **single moments of distinct cultures clashing**, he sets the scene for multiple dramas, which all revolve around bias and the abuse of power in a **metropolitan society,** in which 'prejudging' instead of 'touching', as in really knowing and living with one another, has fatal consequences.

Mural in downtown L. A.

Vocab

Los Angeles inner city life	
Angelenos	name given to the inhabitants of Los Angeles
district **neighborhood** **community**	*Stadtteilbezeichnung in Los Angeles*
boulevard (Bd) **highway (Hy)** **avenue (Av)** **drive (Dr)** **street (St)**	*Straßenbezeichnungen in Los Angeles*
communities working class/immigrant communities community/neighborhood recreation center	*Gemeinden/Stadtbezirke*
crime homicide/rape/aggravated assault/robbery/arson/carjacking/corruption/officer-involved shootings/organized crime	*Mord/Vergewaltigung/ schwere Körperverletzung/ Raubüberfall/Brandstiftung/...*
inner-city life/unemployment/ crime and violence/poverty/ neglect	*innerstädtisch*
LAPD	Los Angeles Police Department
metropolitan area	*Großstadtgebiet*
racial profiling become a victim of racial profiling by police/government agencies	law enforcement practices *(Strafverfolgung)* that disproportionately target people of color
residential area	*Wohngebiet*
urban/suburban population/area/segregation visible in the distinct cultures, values and lifestyles of different neighborhoods	*städtisch/Vorstadt*

transit systems extensive system of bus and subway lines	*öffentlicher Nahverkehr*
welfare programs dependent on welfare live off welfare	*Sozialhilfe*

The plot

In his **episodic, multi-linear drama** *L.A. Crash*, director Paul Harris allows **several intertwined stories** to unfold involving **distinct characters from different social and cultural backgrounds**. Over a **two-day period** in **Los Angeles**, the lives of these characters, although normally separated, become **interconnected by chance encounters**, in which the people involved collide and suffer negative consequences, which in some cases are even irreparable or fatal.

Watching this film, we as viewers,

- learn about fear and aggression caused by racial bias,
- watch worry and frustration turn into contempt and harassment,
- apprehend that change for the better begins with admitting failure,
- see how political ambition makes a travesty of justice and the truth,
- understand how social disadvantage and criminal behavior interconnect and
- realize both the potential, but also the limitations of human bonding.

Through it all, we **analyse** and **evaluate**. However, even more so than the characters on screen, we **confront our**

own individual stereotypical judgments of people and their actions, thereby recognizing that the film is also about us.

Scene-by-Scene analysis

1 Main titles/frame of reference

Opening credits sequence

Two police investigators, the African-American detective Graham Waters and his Latina colleague Ria, have an accident on their way to a murder scene. A Korean woman blames Ria for the accident. While the two women are quarrelling, Waters approaches the crime scene of a 'dead kid', where he kneels down and examines the victim's shoe.

I think we miss that touch so much that we crash into each other just to feel something. (Graham Waters)

Graham, we were rear-ended. We spun around twice. Somewhere in there one of us lost ou frame of reference. I'm gonna look for it. (Ria)

Stop in middle of street! Mexicans! No know how to drive! She blake too fast! (Kim Lee)

1 In your eyes, the opening scene creates, above all, an atmosphere of

▢ anger	▢ disaster
▢ prejudice	▢ frustration
▢ death	▢ mystery

2 Which element of the opening scene determines this atmosphere for you?

▢ snowflakes	▢ instrumental music
▢ blurred lights	▢ dripping sound
▢ unfocused images	▢ Waters' commentar

2 Blind Fear

- Los Angeles during daytime
- Farhad, an ill-tempered man of middle-Eastern appearance, and his daughter, Dorri, attempt to buy a gun and get into a yelling match with the store owner, who repeatedly makes racist remarks. Dorri finally buys the gun and a box of bullets.
- Two young black men come out of a restaurant, arguing about racial discrimination. Reacting to what one of them judges to be a sign of racial prejudice in the gesture of an obviously-rich, white couple, the two of them force this couple out of their car and race off with it.

You, Osama!
Plan your jihad on your own time.
(Gunshop Owner)

I am American citizen! I have right to buy gun!
(Farhad)

We are the only two black faces surrounded by a sea of over-caffeinated white people patrolled by the trigger-happy LAPD. (Anthony)

3 Note the director's work.

- A **bird's-eye shot** introduces Los Angeles as a typical and unremarkable downtown setting
- **Matching cuts of doors** serve as **transition** from one scenario to the other
- **Close-up reaction shots** draw the viewer's attention to the **emotions** visible in the faces of the characters (the spiteful gunshop owner, the increasingly-frantic Farhad, Dorri fighting to maintain control of the situation)

- **Pace** is accelerated in the **four-take reaction shots,** staging the **rising aggression** (Anthony, Peter) and **panic** (Jean and Rick Cabot) in the carjacking incident

3 A Nice Gun

- Anthony and Peter continue arguing in the stolen car.
- The detectives Waters and Ria arrive at a crime scene, where a white cop has accidentally killed a black cop in a drive-by shooting.
- A Mexican locksmith, Daniel Ruiz, is changing the locks on the front door of an expensive-looking house. Jean Cabot, still in shock after the carjacking incident and reacting to the locksmith's tattoos and obvious Hispanic background, becomes hysterical and makes derogative remarks about him. Her husband, Rick, meanwhile is more interested in discussing with his African-American assistant what impact the carjacking incident might have on his "black vote".

... If a white person sees two black people walking towards her and she just happens to turn and walks in the other direction, then she's a racist!

... Your amigo in there is going to sell our keys to one of his homeys and this time it would be fucking great if you acted like you gave a shit! (Jean Cabot)

Why did these two guys have to be black? ... No matter how we spin this, I'm either going to lose the black vote or I'm going to lose the law and order vote! I got West Side Jews up the ass; aren't there any Hasidic kids going bad? (Rick Cabot)

1 What's your idea? While watching the film, you might want to look out for:
- how characters are introduced to the viewer (technically through camera angles and movement, but also by use of text)
- how the car is showcased as a status symbol (i.e. type and function of cars, camera angles)

2 Note the director's work.

- **Tracking shots** showing first her legs and then the upper part of her body **introduce the character** of Jean Cabot bit by bit as a woman who is
  - used to giving orders to people she 'looks down' on (POV shots when descending the stairs; close-up of Daniel Ruiz's tattooed neck and shaven head) because she is wealthy and white (medium shots showing aspects of her expensive-looking house),
  - seriously dissatisfied and discontented (camera zooming in on Jean's facial expression).
- **Over-shoulder reaction shots involve the viewer** in the argument between Rick and his nagging wife Jean by accentuating Rick's consternation and ineffective efforts to calm her down.
- The scene ends with **close-ups** of Jean, Rick and Daniel, **showing the consequences** of Jean's racist comments.

4 Sobriety Test

- Two Asian men are finalizing a business deal inside a diner.
- At the same diner; a white police officer, John Ryan, is talking on a payphone to Shaniqua Johnson, an African-American health insurance official. When she insists that she cannot help him with his father's health problems, he offends her by making presumptions about her ethnicity based on her name. So she hangs up on him.
- Officer Ryan joins his partner, Tom Hansen, in the car and after receiving a report about a stolen car, they pursue a black SUV. Although the car has a different license number, Officer Ryan decides to pull it over to make a random check on the African-American couple – Christine and Cameron Thayer. After first unnecessarily subjecting the husband to a sobriety test, he moves on to frisk the wife in a sexually suggestive way, while his obviously disgusted partner and the woman's helpless husband have to watch the humiliating body search.
- Back in their car again, Christine refuses the appeasing gesture of her husband.
- Officer Hansen, stunned and disillusioned, returns to the squad.

Call any big company with a problem; why is the person you have to deal with guaranteed to be black and stupid? Why? Because corporations are smart. They actually seek out the stupidest fucking black people they can find. They want us to get so frustrated that we'll go away and they won't have to spend their fucking money.
(Officer John Ryan)

Don't you ma'am me! I'm not your fucking mammy.
(Christine Thayer)

We're .. sorry. We'd appreciate it if you'd ... just give us a warning.
(Cameron Thayer)

Note the director's work.

- **Tracking shots** of the Asian leaving the diner after finishing his business deal and a **close-up** of him in his white van frame the scene which **introduces Officer Ryan**; here the viewer's interest is drawn to two scenarios which could plausibly be connected (an illicit business deal and a police officer), but which, despite the many interconnecting stories in the film will not actually be intertwined.
- **Close-up reaction** shots depict a son worried about his father's health (Ryan) and an overworked insurance representative (Shaniqua Johnson); these are designed to help the viewer to better **understand the behavior of both characters.**
- A **high-angle shot**, blurred lights and music frame the scene in which **Ryan abuses his authority** to frisk an African-American couple:
  - **close-ups accentuate the characters' emotions:** doggedness, callousness (Ryan); fear, shock helplessness (Cameron); spite, disgust, humiliation (Christine); distance and disapproval, but also passivity (Hansen)
  - **quickly-edited reaction shots** involving all of the characters **stress the rising tension and a climactic tone**. This culminates in reaction shots that are alternated with inserted close-ups of Ryan's hand grabbing and carressing Christine's body in a sexually suggestive way. The reaction shots focus on Ryan, whose eyes are fixed on Cameron's growing humiliation, on Hansen and Cameron who are both shocked and disgusted, but seem powerless to stop what is happening, or on Christine, who has become degraded to a mere pawn in Ryan's game.

5 A Little Anger

- An older woman wearing a head scarf, who is obviously the Iranian-American store-owner's wife (Shereen), calls out to her husband that the back door of the shop is not closing properly. Dorri loads the gun which her father puts into a drawer underneath the cash register.
- Christine and Cameron argue over how he should have reacted after realizing that his wife was being molested by the white police officer.

That man could have killed your mother. You think I should let crazy people do what they want to us? (Farhad)

Closest you ever came to being black was watching the Cosby Show. (Christine Thayer)

At least I wasn't watching it with the rest of the equestrian team. (Cameron Thayer)

Note the director's work.

- An **establishing shot presents Farhad's shop** as a run-down place (brownish colors, disorganization), where people can get anything from groceries to sunglasses.
- The viewer realizes that Farhad switches constantly between English – the language that is somewhat more naturally used by his wife and daughter – and Farsi, which obviously helps him to vent his anger.
- **Reaction shots** are used to **focus** on Christine's contempt and anger in response to Cameron's resignation and passivity (in contrast to Christine, he does not move about very much in the scene).
- **In a sequence of medium shots, the viewer has the chance to judge the characters**, while watching the

scene through three large, framed windows. These frames have the effect of accentuating how Cameron's lack of passion confines his wife's dignity.

6 Invisible and Impenetrable

Daniel returns home in his white, company-owned van and finds his young daughter, Lara, hiding under her bed. She has been scared by the backfiring of a truck, which she took for gunshots. To make her feel safe, her father mimes putting on a special protective cloak, which he says was given to him by a fairy when he was her age. As he is leaving her room, his beeper goes off, and he drives off with his van again.

> We moved outta that bad neighborhood, not too many guns round here. … It means nothing bad can get through it. Not bullets, nothing. And she says I should wear this cloak and nothing will ever hurt me.
> (Daniel Ruiz)

▷ What's your idea? Which aspect do you feel is most effective in portraying Daniel Ruiz as the total opposite of an aggressive gang member.

- ▢ the **establishing shots** which show that Daniel's house is in a decent, suburban neighborhood and that his daughter's room is decorated in a lovely way.
- ▢ the **low-angle shots** as Daniel crouches down to look under the bed and speaks to his daughter in a gentle and caring voice.
- ▢ the **eye-level** shots in which the viewer sees Daniel putting himself in his daughter's position while he is telling her about the invisible cloak.
- ▢ the way the camera captures the kind and caring expression on his face, but not his tattoos or shaven head
- ▢ the soft music in the background

7 A Personal Problem

- Anthony and Peter are talking about rap versus country music and black activism while they are driving the stolen SUV, when they accidentally run over an Asian man. Not sure what to do at first, they finally pull him out from under the car and take him with them.
- Officer Hansen asks his African-American superior, Lt. Dixon, for a transfer, but he refuses to grant Hansen's wish and explains that a report would only put both of their careers at risk.
- Anthony and Peter drop the injured Asian man at the entrance of a hospital emergency ward and drive off.

No, you want to listen to music of the oppressor, you go right ahead. (Anthony)

This better? You like this? Man's singing about lynchin' a nigga. (Peter)

Just like you probably understand how hard a black man has to work to get to, say, where I am, in a racist fucking organization like the LAPD, and how easily that can all be taken away. But that said, it's your decision: you can put your career and mine on the line in pursuit of a just cause … (Lt. Dixon)

1 Note the director's work.

- **Close-up reaction shots use a slight low angle to direct the viewer's attention** to Anthony's mouth during his tirade and Peter's mouth as he responds to him. This serves to highlight how exaggerated Anthony is in his vehemence when it comes to his favorite subject of racism and to show the light-hearted irony with which Peter questions Anthony's beliefs.
- The **medium shots** of Lt. Dixon and Hansen unobtrusively show the sort of prized objects in the background (e.g. certificates, picture of California's Governor, trophies, etc.) that are characteristic of the office of a typical police lieutenant.
- Both the poster behind Hansen, which is ironically titled "Integrity" and shows the U.S. Presidents in the Mount Rushmore sculpture, and the dividing wall behind Lt. Dixon, which is made up of hollow blocks that are reminiscent of pigeon holes[1], have a symbolic effect: whereas Hansen is trying hard to do what he feels is right (integrity), Lt. Dixon has resigned himself to the widespread racism and "pigeonholing" that exists in the system and which he considers to be an unalterable situation.
- The sequence of 4 **close-ups** (emergency entrance of a hospital, the injured man being thrown from the van, the black SUV and a nativity scene …) creates an ironic effect by reminding the viewer that Anthony and Peter's 'good deed' is not motivated by human kindness, but instead by Peter's warning that they could end up facing an impending murder charge.

---

[1] **pigeon hole** (literal meaning) a small compartment for storing or filing papers, personal possessions, etc.; (figurative meaning) a neat and simple category, which usually fails to reflect the actual complexities involved

2 What's your idea?

- When you hear the hip-hop music introducing this sequence, which of the characters do you spontaneously associate it with? What are your associations with country music? In particular, think about what you believe a certain type of music can say about the people who listen to it regularly.
- When Anthony and Peter realize that they have just run over a person on the street, are you as a viewer more interested in the victim or in what the two of them will do in this situation? Explain whether you find the technical effects used here irritating (x) or effective (✓):

  - ☐ inserted close-up (CU) of key dangling from white van
  - ☐ with the exception of one close-up shot showing the accident victim asking for help, the viewer sees only Anthony and Peter's actions and expressions (reaction shots)
  - ☐ country music playing softly in the background
  - ☐ the victim's groaning sounding like a baby's whimpering

8 Locked and Loaded

- Daniel replaces the lock of the back entrance door to Farhad's shop but advises him to change the door completely as it is not closing properly. Unfortunately, Farhad misunderstands his advice and accuses Daniel of trying to cheat him. The locksmith decides to do without the money Farhad owes him and leaves.
- Anthony and Peter hope to sell the stolen SUV at a chop shop garage, but the owner refuses to accept it because of the blood stains from the accident.

- Detective Waters and his partner Ria are interrupted while making love because his mother calls. Provoked by Graham's racist remarks about her ethnic background, Ria storms off angrily.

> You gotta keep everybody at a certain distance, don't you? What happen, you start to feel something and panic? ... "You want a lesson? How about geography? My father is from Puerto Rico, my mother is from El Salvador; neither one is Mexico."
> (Ria)

> ... so, then I guess the big mystery is: who gathered those remarkably different cultures together and taught them all how to park cars on their lawns?
> (Graham Waters)

1 Note the director's work.

Throughout the film, Haggis makes a point of proving how appearances can be deceiving. In the scenes of chapter 8, he creates an ironic contrast between what colors generally connote and how they accentuate the motif of each particular scene:

- Daniel's dispute with Farhad is filmed with a bluish tint, although *blue* usually suggests trust and confidence.
- Graham and Ria's interrupted lovemaking is set in *brownish colors*, despite the fact that, instead of support and understanding, there is an atmosphere of superficiality and frustration.

2 What's your idea? Use the explanations on pp. 16–17 to look at how colors are used in chapter 9.

9 Taking the Bus

- John Ryan is trying to take care of his father, who obviously has serious prostrate problems.
- Farhad discovers that vandals have broken into his shop via the faulty door and have caused a serious amount of damage.
- District Attorney Rick Cabot and his assistant Karen discuss the investigation into the shooting of the African-American detective by another cop from the LAPD.
- Anthony delivers a monologue to Peter about evil young black men who steal.
- Jean Cabot complains to her maid about not fulfilling her duties because she failed to empty the dishwasher and put away the mugs.
- Because their car will not start, Peter wants to simply take a bus into town instead, but Anthony refuses claiming that 'bus windows humiliate people of color'.

> The man steals from black people. Only reason black people steal from their own: 'Cause they are terrified of white people. ... You have no idea, do you? You have absolutely no idea why they put those great big windows on the sides of buses? One reason only: to humiliate the people of color who are reduced to riding on them. (Anthony)

Note the director's work.

- **Mise en scène:** John Ryan is depicted in semi-darkness in a sparsely-furnished bedroom which lacks personal décor. The light is on in the bathroom where his father's medical condition becomes obvious as does the fact that Ryan's life is focused on taking care of his ailing father.

- The scene in which Farhad discovers that his shop has been broken into works **without dialogue**; the viewer follows Farhad's steps (tracking close-ups of feet), hears the sound of glass crunching under his feet until he realizes the full extent of the damage (wide shot on the chaos in the shop.) The scene is accompanied by melancholic soprano music.

10 Ringing False

- The film director Cameron Thayer has to reshoot a scene because one of the producers wants the actor to 'speak more black'.
- John Ryan initially asks the insurance official Shaniqua Johnson politely for help, but then gets upset and starts making racist remarks, because he is frustrated by the fact that his father seems trapped by the health care system.

Do you know what I can't do? I can't look at you without thinking of the five or six better-qualified white men who didn't get your job. ... You don't like me? Fine, I'm a prick. But my father doesn't deserve to suffer like this. He was a janitor, struggled his whole life, saved enough to start his own company. Twenty-three employees, all black. Paid them equal wages, when no one else was doing that. Forty years he worked side by side with those men, sweeping, carrying garbage. (Ryan)

Have you noticed – this is weird for a white guy to say – but have you noticed that he's talking a lot less black lately? (Fred)

1 Note the director's work.

- The **circling camera**
  - first presents the set of an ethnically-diverse Hollywood studio crew in which the influential people are all white except for Cameron Thayer
  - then zooms in on Cameron realizing the serious tone of his producer.
- **In an over-the-shoulder shot, the viewer takes on Cameron's perspective**, as he listens to his producer's degrading request.

2 What's your idea? **Reaction over-the-shoulder** and **POV shots at eye-level** track the argument between Ryan and the insurance department representative, Shaniqua Johnson. Which emotional reactions can you detect in their faces?

☐ anger	☐ frustration	☐ scorn
☐ disgust	☐ irritation	☐ sympathy
☐ exasperation	☐ desperation	☐ …

11 Brother's Keeper

- While his wife is cleaning up the mess in the vandalized shop, Farhad tries to find out details about Daniel from his firm because he blames the locksmith for the destruction of his store. Dorri is relieved that the gun is still in the drawer.
- Graham Waters visits his mother Louise in her apartment, who wants him to find his brother who is missing. It is obvious that she is a drug addict and Graham has to help her to bed. Back in the car, he lies to his partner Ria, claiming his mother was not in.

They think we're Arabs.
When did Persians become Arab?
(Farhad's wife Shereen)

1. Note the director's work.

- Once again *opening doors* are used as a **transition** to focus on the difference between the mildly empathetic, but annoyed and exasperated Shaniqua Johnson, and an obviously disinterested and slovenly dressed secretary in the firm that Daniel Ruiz works for (Compare also the **mise en scène** of the two offices.).
- The camera moving over framed photographs depicting images of a happier family life in the past captures Waters' hand gently playing some of the keys of the piano before carrying on to show leftover food and drug paraphernalia on the table.
- The inside of the room is bathed in soft light, which creates a sharp contrast to the harsh daylight outside, where Waters then finds his mother sitting in a chair in front of the house.

2. What's your idea?
Throughout the scene, Waters seems detached, his features unreadable. How do you think he actually feels?

☐ angry	☐ discouraged	☐ nostalgic
☐ contemptuous	☐ disgusted	☐ sorry for his mother
☐ defeated	☐ miserable	

12 Uninsured

- At the film studios, Christine approaches Cameron once more to get him to talk about what happened to them during the incident with the police.
- While cleaning up his store with his wife and daughter, Farhad finds out that the insurance company will not cover any of the damage because he failed to have the door properly repaired.

I know what you did
was the right thing, I know that, but …
I was humiliated … for you. I couldn't watch.
I couldn't stand to see that man
take away your dignity.
(Christine Thayer)

Note the director's work.

- The **sharp contrast** between the warm lights of the studio suggesting the world of Hollywood dreams and the harsh light that streams in as the wall of the set is taken away, revealing Christine standing behind it, is used to re-focus the viewer's attention on the unresolved conflict that is currently separating the couple.
- In the following **overhead shot** that shows them walking through the studio, they look just like any other couple having an everyday conversation. As their discussion escalates again, the **camera zooms in**, allowing the viewer to again judge who is right by looking at their argument at **eye-level in a series of reaction shots**.
- There is also **symbolism** in the way they part: the walls on either side of the path that Cameron walks also suggest a corridor that is narrow and restricted, just like the

views that he is holding onto, while Christine, in her frustration, is facing a brick wall both literally and figuratively.

- When Farhad comes to understand that he may have lost everything he owns since the insurance company will not cover the damage to his shop, he stays surprisingly calm, but **low angle shots** express Dorri's worries and raise the viewer's suspicions that the drama is not over yet.

13 Trust

- At the police station, Officer Hansen has to face his former partner's wounded pride and the mockery of his colleagues.
- Graham and Ria are informed that a large sum of money was found hidden in the car driven by the black police officer who was shot.
- Cameron is watching his actors at work but is obviously lost in thought.
- Farhad finds Daniel's bill in the garbage.
- Arriving at the scene of a highway accident with his newly assigned partner, John Ryan rescues Christine from her burning car.

Look at me. Wait till you've been doing it a few more years. You think you know who you are? You have no idea.
(Ryan)

1 Note the director's work.

- **Tight shots** focusing on the characters' faces, with **inserted CUs** of Ryan not letting go of Hansen's hand, make the advice that he gives Hansen sound threatening. This is further emphasized by the background music.

- Synthesizer music blending into a Farsi tune, indistinct voices or sound in the background and a somewhat erratic juxtaposition of single scenes in **high and low angle shots with inserted CUs** connect the first 4 scenes of this chapter in which the characters (Graham and Ria, Cameron and Farhad) seem to be moving toward a decisive moment.
- Soothing synthesizer sounds return as a **wide shot** shows the scene of a road accident and the viewer observes Ryan approaching an overturned car.

2 What's your idea? The scene in which Ryan saves Christine Thayer's life has an almost surrealistic feel to it, and is definitely not as suspense-packed or tumultuous as is usual in action films. Which aspects of the scene contribute to creating this surrealistic feel for you personally?

- ☐ the music alternating between synthesizer music and Farsi singing
- ☐ the contrast of Christine and Ryan's screaming with the music
- ☐ the suppression of the overall sound to a large extent
- ☐ smooth POV shots filmed with a handy cam without blurring effects
- ☐ Ryan's efficient and professional way of handling the situation
- ☐ the predominant brownish color scheme
- ☐ elements of slow motion
- ☐ wide shots of the scene of the accident taken through a cracked windscreen

14 On a Gut Level

- The District Attorney's P.R. manager, Flanagan, believes he has an attractive offer for Detective Waters. If Waters agrees to ignore the controversial incident, his brother's criminal record will be cleared and Waters will receive a good promotion. After initially refusing to play along,

Graham Waters eventually agrees to the plan for the sake of his brother and does in fact withhold the crucial additional evidence when he talks to District Attorney Rick Cabot, even though it means letting an innocent man take the fall.

- While waiting in his car for Daniel to come home, Farhad observes how Lara is kissed and hugged by her mother when she arrives home from school.

It's a warrant for your brother's arrest. Twenty-something years old and already his third felony. Three Strikes Law. Kid's going away for life for stealing a car. Christ that's an unfair law. But still, he had every opportunity you had. Fucking black people, huh? (Flanagan – Rick Cabot's P.R. Manager)

So to make this disappear, all I have to do is frame an innocent man. (Graham Waters)

Note the director's work.

- While Waters is considering Flanagan's proposal, **white light** coming from wall lamps is used to sharpen his profile, which otherwise blends in with the dark paneling of the walls. In a way, these walls seem to absorb Waters (suggesting that he is being pressurized into the deal and absorbed into the system) while Flanagan is connected to the harsh white light of outside reality (suggesting that he knows how to play the game).
- When the viewer sees Waters delivering his answer to the District Attorney in the corridors, the blinding white light falling in through the windows behind him blurs the features on his face. Ironically, white, which is often associ-

ated with truth and innocence, becomes the dominant color, but in this case, it emphasizes that corruption has won out.

- Watching Rick Cabot and his assistant walking away from the camera towards the press conference room and seeing the doors being closed behind them, it becomes clear that neither we as viewers nor Waters himself is going to enter that space in which criminal deals are turned into political truth.

15 Breaking Point

Lost in thought while waiting at a Stop sign, Cameron is suddenly confronted by Anthony and Peter, who try to force him out of his car in order to steal it, but he soon turns the tables on them and assaults the two would-be thieves instead. When police sirens can be heard in the distance, Peter escapes on foot, whereas Cameron drives off with Anthony still sitting in the front passenger seat and then snatches the weapon from him. A dramatic car chase with police officers in pursuit, one of whom is Officer Hansen, finally ends when the SUV is cornered and Cameron is forced to pull over in the driveway of a suburban house.

▷ Note the director's work.

- **Below shots** stage Cameron as the **victimizer**, whereas **high angle shots** portray Anthony as the **victim**.
- **Quick cross-cuttings** between reaction shots at eye-level stress the similarities between Cameron and Anthony while they are frantically exchanging the f-word in the car.

16 Threatening Gestures

Cameron is over the edge, and with Anthony's gun hidden in his waistband, risks being shot when he starts abusing the police officers and refusing to follow their orders. Officer Hansen, who recognizes him from the incident with his former partner, stands up for him and tries to calm him down, and then persuades the other police officers to let Cameron drive away with Anthony still in the car. Soon after, he drops the black youth off on a random boulevard, and reprimands him by expressing his disapproval of how Anthony lives his life, but nevertheless hands the gun back to him.

You embarrass me.
You embarrass yourself.
(Cameron Thayer)

What's your idea? The following techniques help to emphasize how over-the-top and absurdly irrational Cameron's reaction is. Rank them in order of their effectiveness.

- ☐ The director picks a residential area as a very unusual location for a car chase.
- ☐ An inflatable Santa first seems to stop, and in the end, wave goodbye to Cameron.
- ☐ The nativity scene on the garage door associates Cameron's frenzied attempt to be tough and courageous with Jesus dying to deliver the world from sin.
- ☐ Cameron obviously has no clue about what he actually wants, just a vague idea of redemption. However, he does not know how to put this into practice because he does not really comprehend who the guilty party is. This is ironically contrasted by the type of car he is driving: a Navigator.
- ☐ The synthesizer music again creates a surrealistic atmosphere, leaving the viewer wondering what it was all about.

17 A Really Good Cloak

Farhad is waiting in his car to ambush the locksmith. When Daniel arrives in his van, Farhad confronts him and accuses him of cheating him. Daniel's daughter Lara rushes to her father's aid just as Farhad pulls out the gun and fires. After a few moments of stunned and anguished shock, Lara speaks and Daniel realizes that amazingly his daughter is not dead. He frantically searches her for possible wounds while carrying her back inside. Lara believes the invisible cloak has saved their lives, while Farhad, confused and bewildered, is left behind on the street.

It's okay, Daddy.
I'll protect you.
(Lara)

Note the director's work

- The scene is introduced by a **POV shot through the rear window** of a car so that the viewer sees Daniel's van approaching from Farhad's perspective.
- **Tracking shots leading to close-ups** focus on the important elements of the scene:
  - an innocent girl from a close-knit and loving family (presents under the Christmas tree, colorful decorations in the house) with good Christian morals (nativity scene),
  - a gun in the hands of a desperate husband and father whose vision is blurred (Farhad in blinding white light), and who has set out to seek revenge against a hardworking and honest family man (insert CU of inscription on car: "24 hours serving all areas") who has done nothing wrong but is in grave danger

- **White blinding lights** again suggest a surreal nightmare.
- The heated exchange of words between Farhad and Daniel takes place against a musical background that forms a kind of surreal contrast, since it is gently melodic and almost soothing. After the shot rings out, this music then seems to absorb and deaden all other sounds, in particular the anguished cries of Lara's parents, until Lara speaks again to reassure her father.
- **Slow-motion shots** accentuate the absolute horror of the situation, which culminates in the **close-ups** of Daniel, his mouth wide open voicing a cry of pain and anguish which cannot be heard
- A **high angle shot** depicts Farhad standing forlorn on the sidewalk in a state of shock while a **wide shot** aligns his look with a U.S. flag hanging from a neighboring house: it seems he cannot comprehend how it could all come to this in the land which promised peace and liberty.

18 Happenstance

- Detective Waters restocks his mother's fridge.
- Having just finished talking to a friend on the phone, Jean Cabot slips and falls down a flight of stairs.

I'm just angry; Yes, at them!
And the police and Rick and Maria and the dry cleaner who ruined another blouse and the gardener who keeps over-watering the lawn and ... I'm angry all the time. And I don't know why.
(Jean Cabot)

Note the director's work.

- While Jean Cabot is talking about being angry all the time, the **reverse angle shot** of her contains a black and red painting highlighting her state of mind (red for anger, black for depression).

19 Miscommunication

- Peter is standing in the cold, trying to hitch a ride.
- John Ryan is driving home and is obviously lost in thought. At a Stop sign, he stares at something to his right until the tooting of car horns prompts him to move off again.
- Officer Hansen stops to give Peter a ride. As Peter gets in the car, he notices the St. Christopher statuette that is attached to the dashboard and smiles. Feeling ridiculed by Peter's smirking, Hansen stops the car and tells him to get out. When Peter reaches for his own St. Christopher statuette, Hansen immediately suspects that he is reaching for a weapon and therefore quickly pulls out his own gun and shoots him on the spot. Realizing too late, that the youth was unarmed and only wanted to show him the statuette, he pushes Peter's body out of the car.

Something else funny? (Hansen)

Yeah, people, man. (Peter)

1 Note the director's work.

- The **soprano voice** that the audience heard earlier is picked up again and links the scenes of this chapter.
- The **blurred lights** leading to a **wide shot** of Peter standing on a downtown boulevard and the neon sign cross to

the right above his head are elements full of foreboding about what is yet to come.

- The glittering lights of L.A. in the valley below become blurred when viewed from the inside of Hansen's car and the lights from the cars passing by seem to sharpen the profiles of the characters or surrounding objects at random.
- **POV reaction shots** allow the viewer to notice Hansen's growing tension while Peter remains oblivious.
- The audience takes on the perspective of bystanders on the road and watches through the rear window how Hansen shoots Peter, with the shot also killing the music for a brief moment.

2 What's your idea? Although Peter is dead, **POV reaction shots** depicting the expressions on both characters' faces seem to continue the conflict. What do they seem to be asking each other? What answers would you have for them?

20 Human Cargo

- Detective Waters reaches the site of what he later finds out is his brother Peter's dead body.
- Anthony, who despite his earlier objections, is sitting in a bus, suddenly sees the van belonging to the Asian man that they ran over when driving around in the stolen SUV. He quickly gets off the bus and drives away in the van.
- A woman, Kim Lee, finally finds her husband, Choi Jin Gui (the Asian man that Anthony and Peter ran over), in hospital. He sends her off to quickly cash a check that he has kept in his locker.

I am speak
English, you stupid cow!
My husband name Choi Jin Gui!
(Kim Lee)

Note the director's work.

- With the **soprano voice** gradually increasing in intensity, the audience returns to the same scene that the film started with, this time in a **high-angle shot moving across the crime scene before cutting down to a close-up** of Peter's shoe.
- By means of a **reaction shot**, the viewer now realizes that Waters did not recognize the shoe until he noticed his dead brother staring at him. For once, the **close-up** reveals a distinct emotion in Waters' face.
- The soprano voice continues, unaffected by the dramas that are unfolding, and seems an almost mocking accompaniment in the scene, in which the viewer observes Anthony peacefully riding a bus, despite his earlier objections, and therefore realizes that Peter's death was doubly unnecessary and senseless.
- The shrill, hyped-up woman from the beginning of the film, who at first appeared quite comic in seeming to comply with every sort of cliché about Asians, allows the viewer to now experience a brief moment of relief – a mini happy ending – when she finds her husband alive in hospital.
- Anthony perceives the suffering and injustice (darkness in the van) of the Asian refugees, who are chained to the van he has stolen, when he looks at them through a grate separating their reality from his.

21 Things to Do

- When Dorri, working as a pathologist in the hospital's morgue, shows Peter's dead body to Graham Waters and his mother, Graham's mother breaks down, blaming him for the death of his brother.
- Dorri finds her father sitting in his shop with the gun in his hands. He tries to explain what happened, calling Lara his 'little angel', but Dorri remains confused and concerned, and therefore takes away the gun and the blanks and puts them in her bag.

> You did. I asked you to find your brother. But you were busy. We weren't much good to you anymore, were we?
> (Waters' mother Louise)

Note the director's work.

- **Below shots in slow-motion** convey Graham Waters' suffering as he is leaving the morgue as well as his inability to reach out to his partner Ria for consolation and support.

22 Connections

- With his assistant Karen at his side, Rick learns about Jean's fall over the phone and promises to be home soon. At her home, Jean hugs her maid and tells her that she is the best friend she has got.
- Officer Hansen burns his car to destroy any evidence that could potentially link him to Peter's death.

- John Ryan tries to comfort his father who seems to be in a lot of pain.
- Rick Cabot returns home.
- Daniel stands at the window looking out while his wife and daughter lie cuddled up in bed.

I shot a little girl. ... She was my firishta. She was my angel. She saved me. She saved us all. (Farhad)

You want to hear something funny? ... You're the best friend I have. (Jean Cabot)

23 Snowfall

- On his way home, Cameron joins a group of young men dancing around Officer Hansen's burning car. He receives a call from his wife Christine and tells her he loves her.
- Graham Waters re-inspects the crime scene where Peter's body was discovered and finds his brother's St. Christopher statuette.
- On a street corner in Chinatown, Anthony sets free a van full of Asian people who seem to be the victims of human trafficking and gives them some money for food.
- Shaniqua Johnson's car is hit from behind in an accident. She gets out and starts screaming racist comments at the drivers.

Come on – come on – come on, this America, time is money. Chop-chop, let's go. (Anthony to the illegal immigrants)

Don't talk to me unless you can speak American. (Shaniqua to the car drivers who hit her car)

The song "In the Deep" connects this chapter and the next. The music starts up as Jean Cabot is hugging her housekeeper Maria.

"Thought you had all the answers … Now you're out there swimming in the deep."

▷ To which scenario do you think these two lines best apply?

- ☐ Jean Cabot, wife of the wealthy and influential District Attorney, who realizes that no amount of material goods can fill the void in her life.
- ☐ Tom Hansen who experiences his former partner's warning coming true: "You think you know who you are? You have no idea."
- ☐ John Ryan, who has gradually lost all belief in administration and authorities, but who has nothing to replace it with.
- ☐ Daniel Ruiz who must accept that his integrity is not enough to control fate and protect his family.
- ☐ Cameron Thayer, who had the courage to embark on a journey of self-discovery, although afraid of what he would find.
- ☐ Graham Waters who finds his basic distrust of human ties confirmed.

24 End credits

Before you have a closer look at the main characters of the film, go through the quotes from the scenes offered in the section above. Reflect on your reaction to the character in question and what that character is saying. How do their quotes relate to their personality? Use the terms given in the table below to express your ideas.

Vocab: Introducing and discussing quotes

When the character …			
admits	claims	denies	refers to
affirms	compares	explains	says
agrees	concludes	implies	states
announces	contrasts	negates	suggests
argues	counters	observes	threatens
asks	criticizes	points out	warns

… it makes me …		
feel angry	wonder	understand
sympathize	agree with	realize
despise	hope	laugh

The Characters and their scenarios

"You think you know who you are, you have no idea."
(Officer Ryan)

In *L. A. Crash*, Paul Haggis demonstrates how in the **challenging world** of today, **moral values** and common decency can vanish into thin air in each and every one of us when we opt for the **wrong choice based on *presumption*.**

From whites to blacks, Latinos or Koreans to American-Iranians, from cops to criminals, and from the wealthy to the poor and downtrodden, all of the **characters** in this film are shown at their best and worst. Haggis aims to show how devastatingly easy it is for anyone, **regardless of ethnicity or social status**, to become a **corrupted hypocrite** or **vindictive racist**. In keeping with this, the message is clear: just because someone is a member of a seemingly oppressed minority, it does not mean that they cannot become oppressors themselves.

Although at first sight all of the characters in this film seem very different because they come from cultures that are far removed from one another, they nevertheless have **two important aspects in common**: they all **live in the same city** and they all have **similar fears and aspirations**. All of them desperately **want to be good and noble** people, but their rational ideas and efforts to live according to these principles are constantly undermined by **prejudice and repressed emotions**. Take the racist police officer, for example, who ends up risking his own life to rescue a woman he molested the day before, whereas his morally upright, but easily panicked former partner kills a 'brother-in-belief' in cold blood and then simply dumps him by the side of the road rather than owning up to his crime.

As the title suggests, these protagonists, who each go through various **trials** which **test their beliefs and character**, *crash* when they are forced to interact with one another, directly and indirectly, through chance and coincidence. We as viewers then watch the **victims** and **victimizers** switch roles. Through this film, we may become more sensitive to **prejudice, rage and betrayal, societal intolerance, discrimination, and moral definitions of character**.

Character analysis

When analysing some of the film's most important characters, you should always try going back to the film to see which impression you have of a particular character in a particular scene. Ask yourself questions like the following to learn as much about a character as you can:

- What does the character think and/or say about him/herself?
- Is the character associated with particular settings or props (personal possessions; clothing → job, status)?
- How does the character typically speak, act and react?
- What strengths and weaknesses does the character have?
- What is the character's background?
- What beliefs and values does the character have?
- How would I describe the character's overall personality?
- What do other characters think and/or explicitly say about the character in question?
- Can I empathize with this character because I am able to put myself into his/her situation?
- Can this character be forgiven for his/her actions because I understand the motivation behind them?
- Does this character develop and change in the course of the film? If yes, what brings this change about? If no, how does this shape my picture of him/her?

When working with the following role descriptions highlight key terms. Then indicate whether you believe the character is primarily a victim or a victimizer by labeling the name accordingly. The following vocabulary box may help you to explain your view.

Vocab

victim	victimizer
(passive voice) (to)	(active voice)
is abused is attacked (verbally, physically) is bullied is embarrassed is exploited is harassed is harmed	humiliates makes fun of manipulates mocks molests takes advantage of (ab)uses inflicts suffering
feels	
defeated, degraded, desperate, disillusioned, embarrassed, frightened, humiliated, hunted, hurt, miserable , nervous, sad, terrified, upset, wounded	creates his/her own reality feels in control is obsessed with power sees him/herself as the victim reacts based on prejudice/ misconception

VICTIM

VICTIMIZER

About victims and victimizers

The film opens and ends with the character of Detective Graham Waters, whose opening lines thus serve as a framing device for the intertwining but independent stories, which all deal with the various **challenges** individuals face when **struggling to make sense of their lives**.

How to connect with others and not get hurt

Detective Graham Waters Laid-back or egocentric?	
self-reliant, committed to his job	• largely disconnected from his lower-class, poor family (drug-addicted mother and criminal younger brother), he is focussed on his career in the LAPD
focused	• deals with the racial prejudices of the law enforcement system impassively so as not to harm his career
laid back, detached	• disillusioned by the problematic interaction between himself and his family, he has forgotten (unlearned?) how to communicate and show true interest in Ria, who is his partner in his job and in life
professional, calm, methodical, sympathetic	• is at first offended and opposed to withholding evidence against a black cop • in the end, sacrifices his professional integrity in favor of helping his brother

Despite having grown up in an underprivileged social environment, **Graham Waters** has managed to advance to the rank of Detective in the LAPD. Fully aware of the racial animosity and corruption that exists within the system, however, Waters has learned to keep his distance from people. Emotionally alienated from his drug-addicted mother and criminal brother, he regards contact with his family as a duty rather than a pleasure, and his relationship with his Latina partner, Ria, seems to be based more on sex than true emotions or affection. Throughout the film, Waters makes jokes and snide remarks about black people, thereby also distancing himself from the very ethnic group that he was born into. When he is confronted with the negative results of abandoning his brother, he lets himself be pressurized into manipulating the results of his investigation in order to provide Peter with the chance to turn his life around and not end up in prison. He does this knowing full well that he is thereby cementing what seems to be an obvious and systematic institutional abuse of power based on racial bias in the city.

Memories of a happier past

This screenshot taken from Chapter 11, *Brother's Keeper,* illustrates Waters' complex relationship with his family. The focus of the audience is drawn to the harsh lighting on the right side of the frame, which has the effect of sharpening the profiles of Graham and his mother, who are outside the house, even though the dark and hazy depiction of the inside of the room takes up two-thirds of the frame on the left. The pictures on the sideboard – memories of a happier past – suggest that something must have happened which destroyed this idyllic situation and caused both the alienation of the family members and Graham's detachment in general.

How to defy racial discrimination

Anthony	Softy or street thug?
articulate poser	• with great eloquence, Anthony continually interprets the behavior of the people around him, falsely believing himself to be the true defender of the black cause
biased, paranoid	• considering himself to be a post-hip-hop gangster in UCLA college student disguise, he believes in the legitimacy of stealing from those who he feels are unfairly privileged • constantly agitated and upset, Anthony manages to see discrimination and racial profiling in everything and everyone
impressionable, responsive	• towards the end of the film, he makes a more upright moral decision in choosing to release the Asian illegal immigrants caught up in a human trafficking racket, thereby ultimately saving lives and showing a capacity for compassion

Peter	His death – tragic or self-inflicted?
interested, informed, conscientious, open-minded	• says he enjoys both country music and hip-hop and is interested in ice-hockey • in contrast to Anthony, he knows how hip-hop relates to black activism • he carries a statuette of St. Christopher – the patron saint of travelers – with him as a lucky charm, ironically to keep him safe from harm

intense, ironic, positive, perceptive	• he plays the part of the listener, who gently and humorously calls attention to the many contradictions and platitudes in Anthony's tirades and blabbering • as Anthony's partner in crime, he subordinates himself willingly to his dominant friend and constantly reacts to situations rather than taking the initiative • despite his criminal record, he has retained a child-like innocence and an optimistic mindset, which enable him to see the world around him in a more optimistic light than Anthony
inconsistent, passive	• neglected by his drug-addicted mother and a brother who has distanced himself from the family, he has never learned to realize his full potential and so plays by Anthony's rules • in doing so, he carelessly builds up a criminal image, which, although it does not really fit him, will eventually cost him his life

Peter (Detective Waters' younger brother) and his good friend **Anthony** are two African-American youths, who come from an underprivileged background. Carjacking from those who they believe to be "rich, white folks" is their way of taking back from society what, in their eyes, society is denying them. Nevertheless, whereas Anthony firmly believes that everybody around him is unfairly prejudiced against blacks, Peter accepts racial bias as a reaction to individual experience and pleads for more objectivity. In a light-hearted and humorous way, he constantly uncovers Anthony's own heavily-prejudiced and clichéd attitudes and tries to show him the extent to which they often conform to these stereotypes themselves. When it comes to deciding between doing what is morally right and saving their own skin, Peter advocates common-sense and compassion.

Similar but different

This medium shot still from the chapter *Blind Fear* shows Peter questioning the logic of one of Anthony's regular rants about other people's racist behavior. The viewer can see how Peter is depicted as slightly smaller, looking up to his friend with an incredulous expression emphasizing his witty remark. Anthony, on the other hand, seems to be charging ahead in his oversized bomber jacket with a contemptuous and determined look on his face. Since the shot is illuminated by Christmas lights, the v-shape of the tree in the background catches the audience's attention. The fork formed by the tree branches can be seen as showing symbolically that, although Peter and Anthony come from similar backgrounds and are both instinctively trying to square things with society, they nevertheless take very different approaches to the everyday realities of life.

How to fill the void in one's life

Jean Cabot Deplorable or hopelessly spoiled?	
egoistical, class/status conscious	• as the wife of the District Attorney, she freely enjoys the privileges and perks of L.A.'s white establishment • not needing to work to earn her living and surrounded by household staff to do the housework, she is used to using money to settle all matters of life
superficial, snobbish, strongly prejudiced	• her bourgeois and racist attitudes are revealed again and again in her extremely bigoted remarks towards different ethnic minorities • her xenophobic fears become shocking reality when two African-American youths threaten her and her husband at gunpoint and then steal their car
lonely, depressed, desperate	• feeling increasingly alienated from her career-obsessed husband, she suddenly realizes that she may have money, but certainly does not have happiness • the carjacking attack and her accident plunge her into a period of crisis, during which she realizes that her Hispanic housekeeper is the only good friend she has

Rick Cabot	**Liberal or without conscience?**
smart, well-informed, professional, ambitious	• as the white, Democratic District Attorney of L. A., he is totally absorbed in his political career • caring only superficially about his wife's post-traumatic anxieties, he immediately focuses on the probable reaction of his voters to the carjacking incident
perceptive, slick, shrewd	• he never allows himself an openly discriminative remark in public as he wants his potential voters to believe he has no racial prejudices • the details of the carjacking incident do not really interest him; instead, he objectively and insensitively discusses how it threatens or could potentially further his career
ambitious, determined, unscrupulous	• precisely calculating the risks of engaging in corrupt practices, Rick abuses his power to manipulate police procedures in a race-related shooting to his political advantage by pressurizing the officer investigating the incident (i. e. Waters) to leave out crucial and potentially incriminating details

As a white District Attorney in a constituency where his key voters are typically African Americans and Hispanics, Democrat **Richard Cabot** continually manipulates racial politics in L.A. in order to protect his position and further his career. When he and his wife are carjacked by two African-American youths, he does his best to downplay the incident, whereas his wife sees herself confirmed in her pessimistic and racially-biased view of the world. As a result of these conflicting positions, the deceptions and insufficiencies in their relationship and the superficiality of their social network of colleagues and acquaintances become apparent. Whereas Rick doggedly continues to pursue his political aspirations, **Jean** realizes that she will only be able to fill the void that she has been feeling with genuine human contact. Feeling lonely and vulnerable, she turns to their Hispanic housekeeper Maria, and admits to her that she is probably the best friend that she currently has.

Intruding

This over-the-shoulder shot depicts a scene at the Cabots' house, soon after Jean and her husband have been carjacked (Chapter 3, *A Nice Gun*). Various props, such as the fireplace, the sofa and the Christmas decorations suggest that this is actually the Cabots' living room. Nevertheless, the viewer, who takes on Jean's perspective, perceives that the people who are present, i.e. Rick and his assistants, have turned it into a conference room to discuss 'business' as Rick's posture and clothing imply (he is still wearing his suit and has his hands in his pocket). Jean seems to be intruding on this scene as she enters the room asking her husband for 'a second of his time' after the traumatic incident they have just experienced. The viewer will realize later that this scene is symptomatic for the spiteful and verbally aggressive way that Jean typically deals with her husband: whereas he is completely absorbed in and fulfilled by his career, she has great difficulties finding any meaning in a life in which every material worry or daily duty has been taken from her. We consequently understand that Jean's racial bias and arrogance are actually a reflection of her deep frustration and dissatisfaction with her life.

How to confront injustice

Officer John Ryan	From villain to hero?
consistently bigoted	• makes racist comments • abuses his authority and molests an African-American woman during a body search • resents the affirmative action privileges granted to African-Americans
frustrated, embittered, lacking self-control	• is unable to stop himself from harassing the insurance representative, even for the sake of his father
child-like, devoted, dutiful, tender son	• lives together with and cares for his ailing father
professional, altruistic, courageous in the face of physical danger	• instantly assesses the situation after an accident and rushes to help where needed • risks his life to save the black woman he molested the day before • multi-faceted character, who acts instinctively rather than based on careful deliberation, largely because he is constantly reacting to massive pressure in his personal and professional life.

Officer Tom Hansen	Racist in disguise?
sensitive, morally upright, polite, lacks assertiveness	• despises and distances himself from Ryan's racist tendencies • feels unable to stop his partner from molesting an African-American woman
honest and loyal	• initially believes he should support his partner no matter what, then wrestles with the guilt of reporting him to their superior
apparently unbiased	• never shares in or makes excuses for Ryan's behavior
easily stressed out and unable to cope	• kills an African-American youth because he misreads his intentions

John Ryan feels great anguish about the pain and suffering that his father is being forced to endure and is frustrated about the repeated refusal of the African-American health-care insurance representative (Shaniqua Johnson) to authorize paying for a more thorough investigation into the cause of his father's problems. Feeling trapped by the system and unable to cope with his anger on a more intellectual level, this white police officer releases his rage in the form of bigotry by abusing his power and victimizing those whom he considers to be responsible for his problems. Still angry about the situation with Shaniqua Johnson, he pulls over a car and conducts an unnecessary stop-and-search check, during which he humiliates a woman (Christine Thayer) by performing an invasive and sexually-suggestive body search, while his sensitive and more idealistic partner, **Tom Hansen** and the woman's husband are forced to stand by helplessly. When Hansen reports Ryan's inappropriate and racist behavior to his superior Lt. Dixon, the latter is not prepared to compromise his high-ranking position in the LAPD to further investigate the incident, even though he also believes it to be a racist organization. In a very ironic twist, Ryan later finds himself saving the same black woman's life when, reacting instinctively, he rushes to help at the scene of a major accident. In contrast, Hansen, who the viewer believes is unbiased and more racially aware, ends up overreacting and killing a black youth (Peter) after his suppressed prejudices and fears are brought to the surface by a harmless gesture.

Communicating

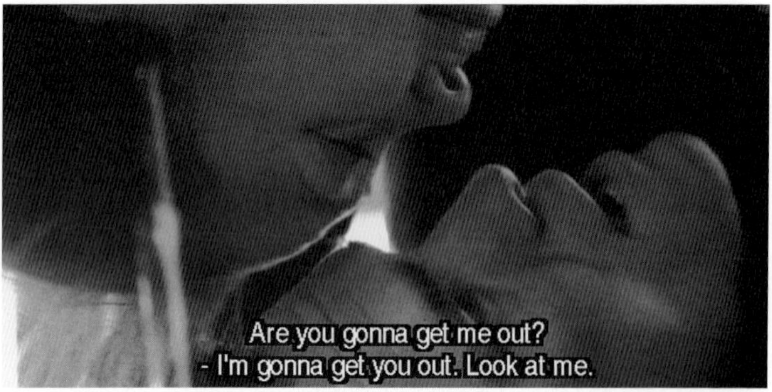

This still is taken from the last scene of Chapter 13, which is entitled *Trust*. It captures the crucial moment when Officer Ryan tries to win back the trust of the woman he molested the night before and who he is now trying to save from an overturned car that is threatening to burst into flames. The close-up shows him making eye-contact and the subtitles let us know that he is also asserting his intention verbally. In order to be able to trust Ryan, however, Christine has to reevaluate who this officer really is: an unscrupulous cop abusing his power and authority or a brave man who means well and has therefore come to her rescue. 'Perceive the other and communicate' as depicted here in this scene is also one of the messages the film conveys in response to the question of how to confront prejudice and violence.

How to reinvent one's identity

Cameron Thayer	
	Naive or cowardly?
ambitious, status/class conscious	• successful Hollywood television director Cameron Thayer is determined to protect his upper middle-class status, even if this means betraying his ethnic background
sensitive, passive, hesitant	• he is clearly in love with his beautiful wife and suffers visibly when she is molested by the police officer • however, he does not believe in his ability to confront situations in which he or his wife are discriminated against based on their African-American background
vulnerable, troubled, anxious, reflective	• his wife's reproaches and the humiliating request he receives from his producer make him more aware of the conflicting stereotypes and prejudices that are eating away at his integrity • all of a sudden, his bottled-up emotions erupt in the form of an almost suicidal rage, which leads him to finally realize how important it is to deal with these complex aspects of his self-identity

Christine Thayer	
	Desperate or vindictive?
proud, self-confident, status/class conscious	• having enjoyed a privileged upbringing, her married life among the affluent black upper-middle class of Hollywood seems happy and fulfilled

fearless, belligerent	• she actively resists Officer Ryan's humiliating body search with verbal aggression and offensive language • even when trapped in her over-turned car, she is at first not willing to accept help from the man who recently molested her but is now trying save her
alert, dynamic, willing to take the initiative	• having realized that her husband does not have the necessary courage to step up and protect her, she impels him to question the value of their privileged, high socio-economic status given that they are still considerably marginalized by bias • in this way, she becomes the driving force which saves their marriage

Having both grown up in a privileged environment, the African-American Hollywood director **Cameron Thayer** and his wife **Christine** are suddenly confronted with the challenge of reevaluating both their priorities in their relationship as well as their status as African Americans in a standoffish and contemptuous white environment. Their marriage is suddenly at stake because Christine reproaches her overly cautious husband for not having intervened to prevent the racist police officer, Ryan, from molesting her during a stop-and-search check. In direct contrast to her husband, she herself reacts to this abuse of power with contempt and aggression, verbally attacking the police officer despite the potential negative consequences. The next day, already distraught and upset by this incident, Cameron realizes, due to a remark made by one of his producers, Fred, that even the show he directs propagates racist stereotypes about black people. Up to this point, Cameron had always believed compliant and adaptive behavior to be the right way to deal with the racist realities around him, even if it often meant sacrificing his dignity and self-respect. When he is finally ready to stand up for himself and for what he feels to be right, his pent-up exasperation and anger lead him to overreact, and he suddenly finds himself cornered by the police after having aggressively confronted the two carjackers (Anthony and Peter). It is only through Officer Hansen's calm handling of the situation that he is able to get out of it unharmed and can later reconnect with his wife.

Betrayal

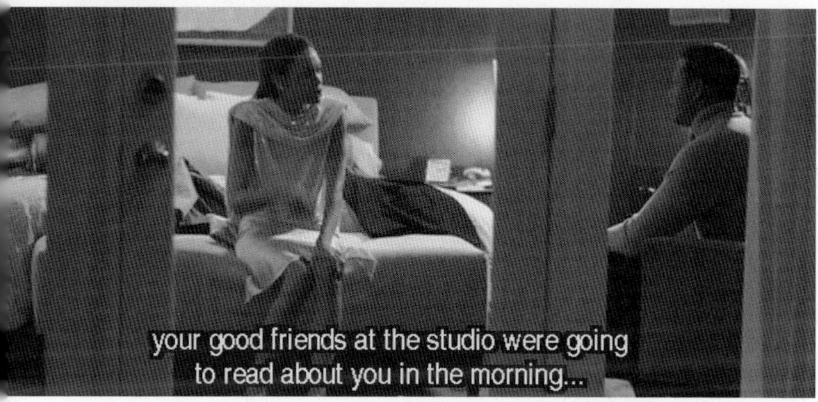

The still from Chapter 5, *A Little Anger*, captures Christine and Cameron Thayer during an argument, in which she accuses him of cowardice and of having betrayed his racial background by not protesting against the officer's molestations during the police stop-and-search. The scene takes place in the intimate environment of their bedroom, thus suggesting that this relates to a fundamental conflict in their relationship. The viewer seems to be holding the camera and filming the scene through the closed glass doors, which divide the frame into three sections: Christine, in the center, is sitting on their marital bed and communicating how the incident and her husband's concerns about what others might think present a challenge to their relationship. Cameron seems unapproachable and unresponsive, confined to just a small amount of space in the section on the right and separated from his wife by a piece of the door frame.

How to find one's place in society

Farhad	**Scapegoat or radical?**
faithful, industrious	• the Iranian-American shop owner works hard to provide his family with a decent life and to support his daughter in her studies
paranoid and mistrustful	• as a result of the climate of distrust following the 9/11 terrorist attacks, Farhad, like many people of Middle-Eastern descent in the U.S., finds himself facing aggressive racist attitudes and hostility • ashamed and defeated, he becomes abusive to everyone around him
touchy, hothead-ed	• his inability to properly communicate in English leads to a misunderstand-ing that is disastrous for his shop and almost fatal for Lara and Daniel • later he regrets his attempt at murderous revenge and is grateful that fate saved him from doing something he would have deeply regretted

Daniel Ruiz	**Gang member redeemed?**
hard-working, honest	• the locksmith of Mexican descent is eager to make a decent living to provide for his wife and daughter • concentrating on his job, he ignores racial and discriminatory remarks from all sides

loving, caring, affectionate	• aware of what fear and mistrust may lead to, he does everything he can to reassure his daughter and provide for her well-being
decent, unbiased, steadfast, blameless	• contrary to what the tattoos on his neck might suggest, he is exemplary in his decency and patience towards others • although he never compromises his integrity, the harmony of his world is constantly threatened by the aggressiveness of other bigoted hypocrites around him

Coming from different cultural backgrounds, Farhad and Daniel Ruiz have in common that they are seeking recognition and financial security in the United States. The Iranian-American shopowner **Farhad**, frustrated by the racial harassment that he and his family have been experiencing and unable to properly communicate in English, feels the need to protect his family and his shop with a gun, and believes that, in doing so, he is acting in line with typical American customs. When he finds himself facing financial ruin after his shop has been wrecked and looted during the night, he consequently, but wrongly, puts the blame on the locksmith (Daniel Ruiz), even though the lock was not the problem. With the gun his daughter Dorri helped him to buy, Farhad seeks to take revenge on Ruiz and only narrowly escapes shooting the locksmith's daughter because the ammunition that Dorri randomly chose in the gunshop turns out to be blanks. Pure chance and blind luck save him and his family from the disaster that his ignorance and obstinacy would have caused.

Daniel Ruiz, on the contrary, seems to be doing better in America. The Hispanic locksmith has moved his family from the insecurities and gang violence of a downtown neighborhood to the promise of greater safety and dignity in suburban L.A.. Although due to his many tattoos and shaven head, he looks like a gangster to people who think in terms of racial and social stereotypes (e.g. Jean Cabot, Farhad), he is actually morally upright and truly good at heart. He is also more familiar with the language, and the American way of life in general, which enables him to move easily and inconspicuously between different social worlds. Knowing that his family is financially dependent on him, he continually sacrifices his personal pride in order to do his job effectively and just get on with it all, simply ignoring the stereotypes and harassment that he is regularly confronted with.

Reparation

This frame is part of one of the climactic scenes (Chapter 17, *A Really Good Cloak*) in the film in which the audience witnesses the tragic consequences of individual demoralization and desperation coupled with mistaken beliefs. Holding the locksmith to be responsible for his misfortune, Farhad has set out to demand compensation for his losses. In an above shot, we as viewers become part of the dangerous threat and are forced to approach the scene with the focus on Farhad's gun in close-up. Daniel Ruiz, who is out of focus, is out of reach for us, so we cannot warn him. The color scheme of the opposing black and white emphasizes the clear-cut difference between wrong and right here. From this perspective, the American viewer might be tempted to question the ideal of the civil liberties allowed by the United States constitution, which make it possible for a man who is so obviously out of touch with reality to own a gun.

▷ In general: When analysing a single frame of a film, you may like to use expressions from the box below and to refer to the technical aspects of film explained in "The language of film from A to Z" (pp. 97–104).

Vocab: Frames

situate the frame within the overall context of the scene or film	This shot depicts/shows/presents/ relates to/portrays … The frame is taken from/is part of/ belongs to …
describe and analyse what the frame shows	There is /are … – The viewer sees/ notices/can identify/detects/looks at/ observes… – in the middle/centre of the picture – at the top/bottom of the frame – on the left/right – in the top left-hand/bottom right-hand corner – in the background/foreground
say which effect is created and how it was achieved	The audience/The viewers have the impression/feel as if/are included in the scene/watch as by-standers/take on the perspective of … The viewer's attention is drawn to/ focused on/divided between …

▷ To finalize this section, draw lines and use the verbs on the following two pages to explain how the characters relate to each other.

How the characters relate

Fred

Cameron Thayer

Christine Thayer

Shaniqua Johnson

Ryan's father

Officer John Ryan

Lt. Dixon

Officer Tom Hansen

Ria

Detective Graham Waters

Louise Waters

loves
manipulates
mediates between
molests
pressurizes
protects
quarrels
refuses
regrets
reproaches
sneers at
subordinates
surrenders to
takes care of
talks … into

Maria
gunshop owner
Jean Cabot
Dorri
Rick Cabot
Karen
Farhad
Flanagan
Shereen
Lara
Daniel Ruiz
Elizabeth

Lucien
Anthony
Peter
Choi Jin Gui
Kim Lee

argue over
asks for
attends
bears with
blames
cares for
do business with
finds consolation
handles
harasses
ignores
is dependent on
is friends with
is united with
keep at a distance
looks down on

The soundtrack

The soundtrack accompanying the film consists of various pieces of music based on synthesizers, in which eerie and haunting voices convey a transcendental atmosphere, and the use of both English and non-English vocals tie in with the film's culturally multi-perspective theme.
In general, music can have various functions in a film. For example, it can be used to …

- set the general mood during the opening credits
- establish the characters' ethnicity, as well as the location, and period of the film
- run parallel to the action
- associate a character with a specific motif; variations of the motif then show different facets of the character and his/her development
- intensify or slow down the pace of a film
- add emotional depth to characters, places, and ideas
- add meaning, particularly if culturally coded

▷ Listen out for the music and other sounds in scenes that you take a particular interest in. Use expressions from the vocabulary box below to explain how you feel these sound elements complement the plot and create atmosphere.

Vocab: Sound and music

shots – police sirens – an explosion – lovemaking – punching – slamming doors/pounding on the door/creaking doors/doors opening/closing – footsteps – telephone ringing – announcements – indistinct chatter in the background – screeching tyres – splintering wood – crunching on a biscuit – breaking glass – fire crackling – a car engine roaring …

The music/sound **(effect)** makes me think of … – evokes images of/an atmosphere of … – brings back memories of … – stirs up a feeling of … – restores peace/tranquility – makes the viewer more alert – is soothing (*beruhigend*)/ exciting/calm/relaxing/frightening – creates a sense of foreboding (*düstere Ahnung*) – lifts my mood/spirits …
The piece of music/**sound** is soft/gentle/romantic/ melodious/raucous (*laut*)/eerie, spooky (*unheimlich*)/ rhythmic/choppy (*abgehackt*)/shrill …
The **singer** has a deep/high-pitched/an appealing (*reizvoll*)/ breathy (*rauchig*)/hoarse (*heiser*)/gentle/penetrating (*durchdringend*)/shrill/strident (*kreischend*)… voice
The **atmosphere/mood** created by the music can be described as romantic/aggressive/threatening/melancholic/ matter-of-fact/…
The **melody** is simple/complex/catchy (*einprägsam*)/ disjunctive (*verzerrt, unmelodiös*) …
There is a slow/fast/simple/complex/steady … **rhythm**
The **instrumentation**[1] consists of strings (*Streichinstrumente*) – woodwind and brass instruments (*Holz- und Blechblasinstrumente*) – percussion – synthesizers …
The **lyrics** talk of/express/relate to/are consistent with the idea of … – contradict – parallel …

As you have seen in the previous sections, the issues that the film *L. A. Crash* deals with include how to:

1. bear failure and frustration
2. handle the feeling of being lost, disconnected
3. find redemption/atonement
4. gain back control and self assurance
5. never give up on yourself and the ones you love
6. overcome self-pity
7. reach out to others
8. restore confidence after beliefs have been shaken unexpectedly
9. stand up against prejudice and stereotypes

[1] For individual instruments and how they sound, you might want to go to: www.imit.org.uk/pages/a-to-z-of-musical-instrument.html

Which lines from the song lyrics below would you choose to match with the main themes of the film? Fill in the numbers from p. 85 accordingly. (The lyrics were taken from songs by Bird York and Stereophonics.)

☐ Thought you had all the answers … but something happens [you] [didn't] see coming

☐ It wastes time and I'd rather be high

☐ Now you're out there swimming… in the deep

☐ Think I'll walk me outside and buy a rainbow smile

☐ Life keeps tumbling your heart in circles till you let go, till you shed your pride

☐ I look around at a beautiful life [in which things have] been the upperside of down, the inside of out

☐ In the silence, all your secrets, will raise their worried heads.

☐ Well, you can pin yourself back together, to who you thought you were.

☐ So maybe tomorrow I'll find my way home

☐ I've been down and I'm wondering why these little black clouds keep walking around with me

Writing a film review

Now that you have watched the film and analysed different aspects of it in detail, it is time to reorganize your findings and render a final judgment of *L. A. Crash* in a personal film review.
To help you with this, a sample review is given below. Read through it and check whether it contains the following relevant elements:

- **general information** about the film's director, actors, ratings
- **brief plot and character description**, taking care not to spoil surprise endings or unexpected plot twists for potential viewers
- **evaluation** of reasons why the reader should go and see the film (or not!)

▷ Mark the passages in which these requirements are met.

Director Paul Haggis bases his award-winning film *L. A. Crash*, set in modern-day Los Angeles, on a personal experience, in which he and his wife were the victims of carjacking.
In the tradition of episodic films from the 1990s, an impressive cast of outstanding Hollywood actors, such as Sandra Bullock, Matt Dillon and Don Cheadle, brings to life the intriguing screenplay which Haggis wrote himself and which deals with hidden preconceptions and everyday racism. Above all, the focus of the film is on its often unpleasant, but always accurately observed characters, whose lives collide *by accident*, bringing everybody's heavily biased perceptions of reality out into the open. Presenting the message

that prejudice and resentment are human, the film does not set out to preach or take a moral stance. Instead, it involves the viewer in the process of decoding plausible explanations for bias and bigotry in order to then condemn even more fiercely the indifference and carelessness with which we accept our own system of intolerance.
This uncompromising insight into destructive human behavior based on everyday stereotypes should not be missed.
The film is rated R for language, sexual content and some violence.

▷ To write a more comprehensive and convincing film review for people your own age, reconsider the list of elements to include that was given above and make use of phrases from the vocabulary grid below. You may also wish to mention particularly striking cinematic techniques (see pp. 97–104) or to comment on the behavior of particular characters (see pp. 62–83).

Vocab: Film review

director
directed by/from the makers of / talented/famous/well-known/acclaimed/skilful/award-winning/Oscar-nominated/revolutionary/controversial …
actors; actor/actress
play/appear in/feature in a lead/major/minor role – talented/(un)convincing – versatile (*wandlungsfähig*)
setting
The action/plot/scene is set in/takes place in/is filmed on location in …
atmosphere
☹ gloomy (*düster*) – dreary – somber – desolate (*trostlos*) – hopeless – haunting (*gespenstisch*) – nightmarish – hostile – threatening – merciless – lonely

☺ bright – luminous – radiant – dazzling – light-hearted – tender – liberating – hopeful – nostalgic – peaceful – welcoming – harmonious – optimistic/pessimistic – idyllic – sympathetic *mitfühlend/verständnisvoll*) – dignified – ecstatic – cheerful

characters/appearance

African American – Asian – Caucasian (white) – Hispanic – of Middle-Eastern appearance – of Mexican descent
brunette – blonde – bald(ing) – shaven head
short – tall – of average height
small/tiny – delicate (*feingliedrig*)/frail (*gebrechlich*) – slim/thin – weak/feeble
large/fat/overweight – heavy/stocky (*stämmig*) – muscular/rugged (*robust*)/strong
pierced – tattooed – scarred (*vernarbt*)
original – unique ↔ stereotyped – (un)believable/flat ↔ well-developed/multidimensional ↔ static
admirable – attractive – enviable – likeable – pathetic (*mitleiderregend*) – repellent (*abstoßend*) …

plot

The film begins with …– The opening scene welcomes the audience to…/In the opening sequence, we see …
The plot/Different scenarios/Single scenes focus on/portray/tell the story of/do (not) come across in a convincing/realistic way …
The plot is based on well-developed ↔ sketchy ideas
The plot structure is complicated ↔ simplistic – full of twists – (un)realistic – suspenseful/thrilling/riveting/gripping ↔ predictable … – Subplots are tied together well ↔ in a confusing way
The film/scene has a tragic/surprising/unexpected/dramatic/satisfying ↔ frustrating ending.
The film/scene contains powerful/striking – (un)convincing/ineffective allusions – metaphors/imagery/symbols/irony
after, afterwards, as, at the same time, before, earlier, finally, first, for a moment, immediately, instantly, just as, last, later, meanwhile, next, soon, then, until

dialogue

comes across as witty/amusing/fast-paced/slow-paced/smart/clever/believable/boring/offensive/confusing/predictable …

reaction

I am impressed by … – I had a hard time understanding/following/watching/listening to …
What particularly surprised me is …
What I liked most is …/To be honest, I did not really like how …
It is rather confusing/frustrating that …
The plot/film is …/The characters/actors are absolutely/not really/in general …
👍 absorbing – clever – dazzling – fascinating – first-rate – intriguing – legendary – powerful – surprising – thought-provoking …
👎 third-rate – ordinary – difficult-to-follow – incredibly tiresome – uninteresting – disappointing – too violent – bloody – predictable – cliché-ridden – outdated – long-winded – slow – boring …

rating

You really shouldn't miss it./It's well worth seeing!/It will definitely change the way you think about …/I strongly recommend it./It is highly entertaining and thought-provoking at the same time./You will be thrilled!/A must-see film!/Amazing/Breathtaking!/Don't waste your time/money!/A film you can('t) afford to miss.

Now that you have worked on many aspects of the film so incredibly thoroughly, it is perhaps time to see how you would do in an exam. To this end, why not tackle one of the assignments from next page?

Good Luck!

Possible exam tasks

Analysis

ABI

1. Examine how *L. A. Crash* explores the theme of fear. Cite examples from the film to illustrate your views.
2. "In the practice of tolerance, one's enemy is the best teacher." (Dalai Lama)

   Interpret the given quote and explain how the film *L. A. Crash* approaches this idea.
3. Analyse the relationships between children and their parents in the film.
4. Punishment, education, love. – Referring to *L. A. Crash*, explain which concept can best help to overcome racial bias.

Composition

1. Compare *L. A. Crash* to another film about race relations of your choice. Explain which one you prefer and why.
2. "One of the things people don't really recognize about the similarities between country and hip-hop is that they're celebrations of pride in a lifestyle." (Taylor Swift)

   Comment on the given quote.
3. Choose a male or a female character from *L. A. Crash* and consider what aspects they would have to change to become a role model?
4. Which actor's performance did you like best? Justify your choice.
5. The producers have agreed to fund a sequel to *L. A. Crash* but on an even lower budget. As a result, certain scenarios have to be dropped and certain characters have to be left out. In a letter to director Paul Haggis, express your ideas about how you would proceed.

Appendix

Vocab: Challenges and choices

The words in each box are closely related, so you may want to look up the exact meaning in a dictionary to understand how their precise meaning and usage.

<table>
<tr><th colspan="2">Challenge</th><th>Consequence
a person may feel</th><th>Reaction
a person may show</th></tr>
<tr><td rowspan="4">be confronted with
encounter
experience
face
suffer</td><td>a catastrophe, a constraint, a difficulty, egotism, hardship, a stroke of fate, trouble</td><td>bewildered, clueless, puzzled skeptical suspicious, uncertain, unsettled</td><td>deal with, grapple with take on, tackle</td></tr>
<tr><td>an accident, arrogance, dominance, intimidation, a loss, a problem, tyranny</td><td>appalled, confused, disconcerted irritated, perplexed, shocked, stunned</td><td>bear, tolerate, wait and see, swallow</td></tr>
<tr><td>a breakdown, a conflict, a contradiction, a disagreement, frustration, oppression, pressure, threat</td><td>beaten, distrustful, exhausted, stressed out, wary</td><td>accept, abide by, concede to, submit to</td></tr>
<tr><td>deprivation, disappoint-ment, (from) an illness, an injury, persecution, strain, stress</td><td>deeply affected, ashamed, embarrassed, humiliated, hurt, troubled, upset, worried, wounded</td><td>call into question, discuss, doubt, hesitate, have qualms about, waver</td></tr>
</table>

Challenge		Consequence a person may feel	Reaction a person may show
be confronted with **encounter** **experience** **face** **suffer**	bigotry, discrimination, injustice, intolerance, prejudice	angry, enraged, furious, insulted, offended, outraged	distrust, harbor suspicion
	defamation, harassment, insult, libel, provocation, slander	in deep despair, depressed, desperate, distressed, downcast, sad, suicidal	confront, defy, fight, stand up to, put up with, withstand
	alienation, animosity, antipathy, hatred, rejection	alarmed, afraid, frightened, intimidated, scared	show contempt for, despise, feel disgust, hate, loathe
	disrespect, contempt, impertinence		oppose, protest, rebel against
	aggression, assault, attack, brutality, cruelty, physical abuse, rape, verbal abuse, violence		refuse to accept, reject, resist

Vocab: Race relations

bias (*einseitige Tendenz*) – be biased against/towards – be aware of – overcome bias and prejudice
bigotry (*Voreingenommenheit*) – bigot – a bigoted person
cultural diversity – culture gap – culture clash – live in a culturally diverse neighborhood

discrimination – discriminate against – discriminatory – practices in social welfare/at the workplace

equality – equal rights – equal opportunity – firm belief in – believe in – fight against social inequality

exclusion – exclude somebody from society

gang – gang member – join a gang – L.A. street gangs – a gang roaming the street

ghetto – ghettoization of inner cities – an inner-city ghetto

harassment (*Schikane, Mobbing*) – harass – harassing – experience – fight against harassment

ignorance (*Ahnungslosigkeit*) – ignorant of – feign ignorance = pretend to be ignorant

integration – integrate somebody into – be integrated into mainstream society

justice – just – contribute to (in)justice – endure injustice

majority ↔ minority– an overall majority – the majority opinion/view – discrimination against minorities

multiculturalism – promote a multicultural society

narrow-minded ↔ open-minded – This indicates (= shows) /is a sign of somebody's narrow-mindedness

prejudice – be prejudiced against – prejudicial behavior – reinforce prejudice within society

race – racism – racist – racial bias – segregation – race riots – escalate – forms of racial profiling – interracial conflicts

resentment against/towards sb. or sth. – resent – growing/ widespread resentment

respect ↔ disrespect – respectful – show one's respect for

right – have the right to – deny somebody the right to – (self-)righteous – advocate equal rights – guarantee/protect (civil) rights

stereotype – believe in stereotypical behavior – stereotyped thinking/think in stereotypes

tolerance of/towards sb. or sth. – tolerate – tolerant – speak up against intolerance – promote tolerance and understanding – show tolerance towards each other – a tolerant society – stirring up a climate of fear and intolerance

xenophobia (*Fremdenfeindlichkeit*) – xenophobic – steadily-growing xenophobia

Vocab: Character description

adaptable
affectionate
altruistic
ambitious
annoying
anxious
arrogant
articulate
assertive
biased
bigoted
blameless
brave
bossy
careful
careless
caring
calm
cautious
childlike
class-/status-conscious
committed
compassionate
complex
compliant
conceited
confident
conscientious
considerate
courageous
decent
defiant
depressed
desperate
detached
determined
devoted
disconcerted
dreamer
dutiful
efficient
egoistical
embittered
energetic
fair
faithful
focused
forgiving
frustrated
fun-loving
generous
gentle
hard-working
heavily-biased
hesitant
honest
hot-headed
imaginative
impressionable
impulsive
independent
industrious
intense
interested
ironic
jealous
judgmental
kind
laid-back
likeable
lonely
loving
loyal
manipulative
materialistic
methodical
mistrustful
morally-upright
naive
open-minded
opinionated
paranoid
passive
patient
perceptive
perfectionist
perturbed
pleasant
polite
poser
positive
professional
profound
proud
questioning
quick-tempered
radical
realistic
rebellious
reflective
relaxed
reliable
reserved
respectful
(ir)responsible
responsive
rigid
rude
sarcastic
self-confident
self-conscious
selfish
self-reliant
sensible
sensitive
serious
shrewd
shy
simple-minded
slick
smart
stable
snobbish
steadfast
strong
stubborn
superficial
successful
tender
timid
thoughtful
tireless
tolerant
touchy
troubled
trusting
understanding
unscrupulous
vain
vulnerable
warm
well-informed
wise
witty
xenophobic
youthful
zealous

Vocab: Emotional reactions

acceptance	empathy	love
admiration	enthusiasm	manipulation
affection	envy	melancholy
aggravation	euphoria	misery
aggression	excitement	mortification
agitation	exhilaration	panic
alarm	fondness	paranoia
alienation	forgiveness	pity
amazement	fright	pleasure
ambivalence	frustration	pride
amusement	fury	quirkiness
anxiety	gloom	rage
apathy	gratitude	regret
apprehension	grief	remorse
astonishment	grouchiness	resentment
attraction	guilt	revulsion
bitterness	happiness	sentimentality
bliss	hate	shame
boredom	hatred	shock
compassion	homesickness	suffering
confusion	hope	sympathy
contempt	horror	tenseness
delight	hostility	terror
depression	humiliation	uneasiness
despair	hysteria	unhappiness
distress	insecurity	violence
domination	interest	worry
doubt	jealousy	wrath
dread	joy(fulness)	yearning
ecstasy	kindness	zeal
elation	loathing	
embarrassment	loneliness	

The language of film from A-Z

For even more terms, go to: www.imdb.com/glossary/

ambiance	The overall mood of a scene or setting	
antagonist	The main character in conflict with the film's hero(ine), lead character or protagonist (also: bad guy, or villain)	
camera angles	camera	purpose/effect
• bird's-eye view • high angle/crane/ overhead shot	positioned above	With high angle shots, the viewer looks down on the action. This makes people and objects appear smaller, less important, or even insignificant, or helps to put them into a larger context.
• low angle/below shot	positioned below	Low angles may make characters look dominant, aggressive, and threatening. If focussed on the action, they will most often create an intimidating atmosphere.
• eye-level/straight-on angle	positioned at eye-level with the viewer or one of the characters involved	Eye-level shots are the most common camera angle as they help to make the viewers feel part of the scene, as if they were confronting the person or object directly. This also makes the scene feel more 'realistic'.
• establishing shot (long or wide shot)	positioned at a distance or zoomed out so that particular objects, the location in general or characters appear relatively small in the frame	Establishing shots usually occur at the beginning of a scene (or a sequence) and help the viewer to identify the location and approximate time of the scene as a form of orientation.

• medium shot (one-/two-/three-shot)	positioned at or zoomed to a medium distance so as to show a human figure from the waist or knees up, depending on the number of people or objects in the frame	Medium shots place the focus on the action/interaction of the people in the frame.
• close-up (CU) • extreme close-up (ECU)	positioned or zoomed in to a close distance so that objects and people or certain aspects of them appear relatively large and fill the entire frame	CUs and ECUs focus attention on something and emphasize its importance; when facial expressions are in focus rather than the external action, it often makes us feel either more comfortable or extremely uncomfortable.
• insert(ed) CU	refers to a shot taken of a static object, which fills most of the frame and is inserted later during the editing process, typically between two shots of a character looking offscreen	Inserted CUs are employed to emphasize a relevant object which could easily be overlooked in the complex mise en scène of the shot and/or to show what a character is looking at.
• point of view shot (POV)	positioned so as to take the shot from the subjective perspective of one of the characters and usually coupled with a reaction shot	POVs are meant to show the audience the scene as if through the eyes of one of the characters.

• reaction shot	refers to a quick shot that records a character's or group's response to another character or some on-screen action or event	Reaction shots help viewers to feel more involved in the dialogue or the action.
• over-(the)-shoulder shot (OTS)	refers to a shot which records the action from behind the shoulder and/or head of one of the characters, who is usually looking in the direction of another character	OTSs help to link the characters involved in a scene by establishing their respective positions. By giving the viewers the impression that they are looking at a person or a group of people from the other person's point of view, OTSs help viewers to feel like they are actually interacting with the other character(s) in the film.
• reverse angle shot/ reverse shot	refers to a shot photographed from the opposite side of a person/object to provide a different perspective	Reverse angle shots are typically used for scenes in which the focus is on the dialogue and character interaction.
camera movement		
• pan(ning)/ tracking shot	camera movement from left to right (or vice versa), with the camera moving on a 'dolly' (a platform on wheels)	Panning/tracking shots are used to follow the action or to survey the overall setting. This gives viewers the feeling that they are part of the scene because they are following the action closely at eye-level.

• tilt (up or down)	camera movement upwards or downwards	A tilt can be used to emphasize the height of something, to simulate someone looking up or down or to surprise the viewers by focusing on a change.
• zoom in/out	refers to changing the framing of a shot from *wide angle* to *close-up* and vice versa	Zooming in serves to isolate a person or object from the surrounding environment and to put it into focus; zooming out is used to place something or someone within a larger context.
camera speed		
• slow motion	a technique which makes people or objects appear to be moving more slowly than normal	Slow motion in films usually builds suspense, intensifies emotions or simply highlights the importance of the moment.
• fast motion	a technique which makes people or objects appear to be moving more quickly than normal	Fast motion usually creates a comic and/or hectic effect.
• freeze frame	a frame image created by stopping the film in the middle of the action	Freeze frames are often used at the end of a film to indicate death, to introduce ambiguity, and to provide an iconic, lasting image.
cast	all of the actors appearing in a film	
credits	list of cast, crew, and other people involved in making a film (*opening credits* appear at the beginning, *closing credits* at the end)	
crew	all those involved in the technical production of a film, who are not actual performers	

critic	a person who publishes a review of a film, considering it from either an artistic or entertainment point of view	
cut	an essential part of the editing process; an abrupt change in camera angle, location or time, from one shot to another	
• cross-cutting	editing technique that combines two scenes or events by alternating between them or interweaving them with one another	Cross-cutting enables viewers to realize that the two actions are somehow linked, and the characters from the different lines of action are connected in some way.
• dissolve, burn-in/-out fade-in/-out	the visible image of one shot or scene is gradually replaced, superimposed or blended in or out (by an overlapping fade-out or fade-in and following dissolve) of the image from another shot or scene	This superimposition of shots is often used to suggest the passage of time or to imitate hallucinatory states.
• match cut	a cut between two shots (outgoing and incoming), which are felt to be "matched" because they contain similar elements	A match cut emphasizes the continuity of the action and helps to link one scene to another more smoothly.
director	a director usually has the complete artistic control over all aspects of the film, such as casting, script editing, shot selection, shot composition, and editing, etc. On the film set, the director is also responsible for communicating to actors how a particular scene is to be performed.	

editing	the process by which the many separate camera takes of the filming process are selected, assembled, arranged, trimmed, structured, and spliced (= joined) together to form a complete sequence in line with the script	
eyeline	the direction in which a character is looking	Eyelines are often a way of letting the viewers know what (or whom) a character is interested in.
focus	refers to the degree of sharpness and clarity in a film image; "out-of-focus": images are blurred and lack clear linear definition	
foreshadowing	refers to hints provided within a film (in the form of symbols, images, motifs, repetition, dialogue or mood) about the outcome of the plot, or about an upcoming action that will take place	This is often done in order to prepare viewers for later events, revelations, or plot developments; ominous music also often foreshadows danger or builds suspense.
frame	a single image of a film	
interior/exterior	a scene apparently shot indoors or out of doors	
lighting	refers to the overall illumination of the set and may be described in terms of the direction from which the light enters the set (front-lighting, back-lighting, side-lighting, top-lighting, cross-lighting) or simply in terms of the contrast between light and dark (high-key, low-key lighting)	
mise en scène	refers to all of the elements within the frame of the film and how they are arranged in front of the camera; includes, for example, the setting, overall decor, props, actors, costumes, makeup, lighting, performances and characters	

pace	the speed/tempo of the dramatic action, which is usually enhanced by the soundtrack and the speed of the dialogue, the type of editing, etc.
plot/ plot point	refers to a series of dramatic events or actions that make up a film's narrative; a plot point is a key turning point or moment in a film's story that significantly advances the action; plot points either move the story forward or disrupt and complicate the plot
producer	a producer is responsible for raising funding, hiring personnel, and arranging the sale of a film to cinemas or the distribution rights for DVDs
props (abbreviation for properties)	refers to hand-held objects, decorations, or any other moveable items that actors use or interact with in a scene
protagonist	the lead or main character in a film; also known as the hero/heroine; contrast to *antagonist*
ratings	also known as the MPAA (Motion Picture Association of America) film rating system, first officially instituted in late 1968; it refers to the ever-evolving classification system for films, usually based upon age-appropriateness, and the judgment of a film's suitability for various audiences in terms of sexual content, offensiveness, or violence
release	refers to the first distribution and general public exhibition of a film to theatre audiences
running time	a measure of the duration or length of a film, usually about two hours for a feature film
script/screenplay	text written to be turned into a film that contains dialogue, as well as first ideas on staging like *mise en scène*, camera movement, etc.
set	in contrast to location, set refers to an artificially constructed environment used for filming
shot	refers to a single image, the smallest compositional unit of a film's structure

sound	 **speech (dialogue)** **music** **noises (sound effects)**	The sound in a film serves to • simulate reality • create illusion • generate the mood Music, in particular, can help to • underline a character's emotions • evoke nostalgic feelings • foreshadow an event • build suspense • establish transitions between scenes • provide the viewer with a tone or an emotional attitude toward the story and/or the characters
tagline	very short summary of a film plot	
voice-over	commentary by an unseen narrator, an off-screen voice or a character whose lips are not moving	The commentary helps to set the theme and often encourages the viewer to look for a deeper meaning in the action on the screen.

Some explanations which might help

Burbank, Santa Monica, Sherman Oaks, Toluca Lake	affluent residential areas of Los Angeles
Compton	working-class neighborhood with a high concentration of gang violence
Cosby Show	popular TV sitcom created by and featuring the comedian Bill Cosby and centering around the life of an upper middle-class African-American family
Discovery Channel	cable TV channel showing documentary television programs focussing on popular science
Greenwich	Bohemian neighborhood of New York
homie	slang term for 'friend from the neighborhood'
Huey Newton, Bobby Seal, Eldridge Cleaver, Fred Hampton	political activists for black rights
jihad	holy war (fought by Muslims defending Islam)
Kings	L.A.'s professional ice-hockey team
Osama	Osama Bin Laden Al-Qaeda terrorist, prime target in the U.S. War on Terror, killed by the CIA in 2011
S.I.D.	Scientific Investigation Division (= CSI)
Saddam	Saddam Hussein former President of Iraq, executed in 2006
Stapes Center	multi-purpose sports arena
The Valley	San Fernando Valley north of the Hollywood Hills wealthy residential areas
Three Strikes Law	statute compelling the court to impose harsher sentences on habitual offenders who have already been convicted twice before

Index

characters 11, 60–83, 89, 95
- Anthony 31f., 38ff., 42, 50f., 55f., 58, 66ff., 77, 83
- Jean Cabot 32f., 42, 53f., 57ff., 69, 71f., 80, 83
- Rick Cabot 32f., 42, 49f., 53, 57f., 70f., 83
- Daniel 32f., 37, 40f., 44f., 47, 49, 52f., 58f., 78ff., 83
- Dorri 31, 36, 44, 47, 57, 79, 83
- Farhad 31, 36, 40–44, 46, 49, 52f., 58, 78ff., 83
- Officer Tom Hansen 34f., 38f., 47, 50f., 54f., 57f., 73f., 77, 82
- Peter 32, 38ff., 42, 50, 54–58, 65–68, 74, 77, 83
- Ria 30, 32, 41, 44, 47f., 57, 64, 82
- Officer John Ryan 34 f., 42ff., 47f., 54, 58ff., 72ff., 76, 82
- Christine Thayer 34ff., 46ff., 58, 73–77, 82
- Cameron Thayer 34-37, 43f., 46ff., 50f., 58f., 75ff., 82
- Detective Graham Waters 30, 32, 41, 44f., 47–50, 53, 55–59, 63ff., 70, 82

cinematic devices 11, 97–104

colors and their meaning 16f., 41

film poster 12–18

film review 87–90

genre 7–10

Haggis, Paul (director) 16, 22, 24, 27, 87, 91

Los Angeles (setting) 20, 24–29, 31, 55, 70, 80, 87, 105

plot 29–59, 87ff.

purpose 7–10

scene-by-scene analysis 30–59

script 10f., 103

soundtrack 11, 84ff., 104

techniques 8, 11, 51, 97–104

trailer 12, 18–21

Acknowledgments

Texts

p. 20: © 2005 Lions Gate Entertainment. All rights reserved; p. 24: Copyright © 2001-2013 BrainyQuote [17.10.2013]

Images

front and back cover: © Universum Film/Cinetext; pp. 6, 8, 10, 13, 14, 21, 23, 30, 33, 37, 40, 41, 44, 45, 48, 51, 55, 59, 60, 62, 63 (top), 81, 84, 86, 88: © incomible – iStockphoto; p. 10: © Big_Ryan – iStockphoto; p. 11 (bottom): © filo – iStockphoto; p. 12: © VladSt – iStockphoto; p. 14: © 2005 Lions Gate Entertainment. All rights reserved; p. 16: © ihorzigor – iStockphoto; p. 22: www.fsk.de/FSK-Kennzeichen; pp. 25, 65, 68, 71, 74, 77, 80: © 2006 Universum Film; p. 27: © Monica Almeida/NYT/Redux/laif; pp. 64 (top), 66, 68, 69, 70 (top), 72, 73 (top), 75, 78, : © carlosgardel – Fotolia.com; pp. 64 (bottom), 67, 70 (bottom), 73 (bottom), 76, 79, : © uncle-rico – iStockphoto; others: Verlagsarchiv Schöningh

Sollte trotz aller Bemühungen um korrekte Urheberangaben ein Irrtum unterlaufen sein, bitten wir darum, sich mit dem Verlag in Verbindung zu setzen, damit wir eventuell erforderliche Korrekturen vornehmen können.